The Amstrad CPC464 Disc System
Including CP/M and Printers

Other books for Amstrad users

Amstrad Computing
Ian Sinclair
0 00 383120 5

Sensational Games for the Amstrad CPC464 and CPC664
Jim Gregory
0 00 383121 3

Adventure Games for the Amstrad CPC464
A. J. Bradbury
0 00 383078 0

40 Educational Games for the Amstrad CPC464
Vince Apps
0 00 383119 1

Practical Programs for the Amstrad CPC464
Audrey Bishop and Owen Bishop
0 00 383082 9

Filing Systems and Databases for the Amstrad CPC464
A. P. Stephenson and D. J. Stephenson
0 0 383102 7

The Amstrad CPC464 Disc System

Including CP/M and Printers

Ian Sinclair

COLLINS
8 Grafton Street, London W1

Collins Professional and Technical Books
William Collins Sons & Co. Ltd
8 Grafton Street, London W1X 3LA

First published in Great Britain by
Collins Professional and Technical Books 1985
Reprinted 1985 (twice)

Distributed in the United States of America
by Sheridan House, Inc.

British Library Cataloguing in Publication Data
Sinclair, Ian R.
The Amstrad CPC464 disc system: including CP/M and printers.
1. Amstrad CPC464 (Computer)   2. Data disk drives
3. Printers (Data processing systems)
I. Title
001.64'4   QA76.8.A4

ISBN 0–00–383177–9

Typeset by V & M Graphics Ltd, Aylesbury, Bucks
Printed and bound in Great Britain by
Mackays of Chatham, Kent

Contents

Preface

Sooner or later the serious programmer will become frustrated with using cassettes, and will turn to disc drives. The good BASIC, the large memory size, and the easy use of machine code of the Amstrad CPC464 all combine to make it very attractive to serious programmers, so it is inevitable that many CPC464 users are acquiring, or intend to acquire, disc systems. The Amstrad disc system, however, is unique to this machine, and its operation is not obvious to a beginner. Even an experienced programmer who has worked with other disc systems may find that the Amstrad DDI-1 is by no means easy to understand. In particular, the presence of both the Amstrad disc operating system and a version of the well-known CP/M 2.2 on the same Master disc is unusual, and the CP/M commands are not explained at great length in the Manual. For CP/M information, the reader is referred by the Manual to a publication which was certainly not available at the time when the disc drives first appeared!

This book is intended as a beginner's introduction to the DDI-1 disc system that is currently available for the CPC464 machine, and which will be used in built-in form on others. By 'beginner', I don't necessarily mean a beginner to computers, but a beginner to *disc* systems. At the same time, I hope that this book will be intelligible and useful to the beginner to computing who has a disc-equipped Amstrad CPC464. This book will concentrate on extended explanations of what disc operation is about, and how to make the most effective use of discs. This is not always apparent to the newcomer to disc systems, even after considerable experience of using the cassette-based machine. I shall not assume, as so many books on disc operation seem to, that the reader is at ease with machine code or hexadecimal notation, so these points will be explained as they are introduced.

The book also covers the use of some of the 'disc utilities' – the programs (which are supplied on disc) which can provide some useful actions for the disc user. To help the disc user further, some listings of my own utilities are provided too.

The beginner generally finds the action of disc utilities very confusing, and so I have included some examples of how such utilities can be of very great help, for example, in reading data from a disc, and in retitling a program without requiring to switch to CP/M. Only a small part of the book is devoted to CP/M, for reasons that are dealt with in more detail in the text. The main reason is that CP/M is likely to be used only as a way of running some specialised programs, not as a way of using the disc with programs in BASIC. At the time of writing, very few CP/M programs were available on the 3-inch disc format.

Since the serious programmer is bound to want to use a printer, I have included a chapter on printers. The printer which is available from Amstrad is reasonably described in its own manual, and I have concentrated on other printers, such as the Epson series. These printers are used extensively both by the more serious programmer and by the business user, and the action of printers such as the Juki daisywheel printer and the Tandy CGP-115 graphics printer has been added. Since combined typewriter/printers can now be obtained at very attractive prices, the buyer should have as wide a choice as possible, and this book describes what is available and how it can be used.

As always, the book owes its creation to a number of people. I would particularly like to thank my long-suffering friends at Collins Professional and Technical Books. Richard Miles commissioned the manuscript, Sue Moore and Janet Murphy performed miracles on my typescript, and the typesetters and printers worked at breakneck speed to bring the book quickly into existence. I am deeply grateful to all of them.

Note: The spelling 'disc' has been used throughout. This is the spelling which is used by Amstrad, as distinct from the US version 'disk'. The difference is important, because the CPC464 disc system will reject the word 'disk' used in a command.

Ian Sinclair

Chapter One
About Discs and Disc Systems

Why use discs

One of the questions that a beginner to computing inevitably asks is – why use discs? The obvious reasons are not necessarily the most important ones. The novice owner will see more clearly the advantages of using discs only after some time spent using cassettes. We'll start, then, by showing why the use of discs is so important for the more advanced programmer and experienced user alike.

To start with, a disc offers *much* faster operation. If you use a machine to load one program, and then use that program (a game perhaps) for several hours, this speed advantage may be of little use. It certainly would not justify the cost of a disc system. On the other hand, if you are developing programs for yourself, you may want to load a program, make changes, and save it again before you try out the new version. This can be very tedious if you have to wait for cassettes to load and save. It's even more tedious because cassette operation is not automatic. You have to either store each version of the program on a new cassette, or use a long cassette (C60 or C90), with each program version noted as a starting point on the tape counter. If you use separate cassettes, you may find yourself holding a dozen of them by the time the program is complete. If you use C90s, you will need paper to note the tape count positions of each version of the program. Either way, it's tedious.

This is particularly true for the machine code programmer who is using the Amsoft DEVPAC of assembler, editor and monitor. Because of the nature of machine code, any fault in a program which is being developed may require the machine to be switched off and then on again in order to regain control. This inevitably results in the loss of the stored programs, so that the MONA3 monitor and the GENA3 assembler have to be reloaded, then the assembly language text file, before the program can be reassembled and revised. Since the DEVPAC programs are large (MONA3 is 7K and GENA3 is 9K) cassette loading takes a long time, and the development of a large machine code program under these circumstances is not really feasible.

Another class of user who will benefit greatly from the use of discs is the text writer. If you use the Amstrad CPC464, as many users do, to create and edit text with the EASI-AMSWORD or AMSWORD 1 text editor programs, then the time that is needed for cassettes to load or save the data is a definite handicap. If you want to load a piece of text, change a few words, and then store the new version, the loading and saving time is a very large part of the total. From experience, I can testify that word processing with cassettes is very little better than using the old-fashioned typewriter, and that the real advantages of word processing are apparent only when a disc system is used.

The overwhelming advantage of using a disc system, however, is automatic operation. The CPC464 cassette system does, at least, permit the motor of the cassette recorder to be controlled, and it allows programs or data files to be referred to by name. If you try to load a program called "TEXINDEX", however, without winding the cassette back to the beginning, you may find that the program cannot be loaded. This is because recording on tape is 'serial' – you start recording at the beginning of the tape, and wind it on to the end. If you then want to load something which is at the start of the tape, you have to rewind it for yourself. The computer does *not* control the actions of fast forward and reverse, because the cassette recorder was not designed for it to do so. The disc system, by contrast, is completely computer controlled. The only manual action is that of putting in the correct disc, and making sure that it is the right way round. On loading, the computer will use its disc operating system to find the program or other material that you want, from its title. Having located the start, it will then load the data into the computer in only a few seconds. Saving is just as automatic. The SAVE command is followed by a filename (and other information in some cases), and pressing ENTER carries out the actions of finding unused space on the disc, and saving the data. The automatic nature of this action also means that a 'catalogue' can be kept on the disc itself. This means that you can insert a disc and obtain information on what is stored on it without the need to play back the whole disc. Though you can also find the names of programs on a cassette you have to *replay a whole cassette* in order to see its catalogue.

In addition to these compelling reasons for using discs, are the extra commands that the disc operating system permits. Some computers go much further in this respect, so that their disc system adds a BASIC of its own. In the CPC464 disc system the new commands are all closely tied to the use of the disc system itself, and we shall examine them in detail. Several of the extra commands, however, allow you to obtain a lot more information about how the data is stored on the disc. This will not be of immediate use to you if you haven't used discs before, but its usefulness will be apparent before long.

Finally, the use of discs can bring order and reliability to what can be a very haphazard business. When you use cassettes for filing programs and data, you inevitably end up with a very large number of cassettes, all of which have to be catalogued. I had over two hundred cassettes at one stage! It can take a considerable time to locate a program on a cassette. Because the CPC464 disc makes use of both sides, it can hold just as much information as the whole of a C90 cassette, and the information is much easier to get at. This encourages you to use the whole of a disc, whereas you might use only the first ten minutes of a C90 cassette. It's quite possible to find, for example, that you can keep all of the programs that you want to use on one single disc! This alone is such a liberation that by itself it almost justifies the use of discs. Discs are slim and compact to store, so that a box of ten discs, holding a huge number of programs, will take up little more space than a couple of cassettes. The reliability of disc recording means that you can make a backup copy of a valuable program, and be fairly certain that you will never need it. Unless you spill coffee all over a disc, demagnetise it or smash through its protective cover, it's unlikely that you will lose a program. Cassettes are *never* so reliable.

What is a disc system

Disc system is the name that is given to a complicated combination of hardware and software. Hardware means the equipment in boxes, software is programming which can be on a disc or in the form of chips that plug into the machine. A disc system comprises the disc drive (or drives), the disc controlling circuits, and the disc operating system.

Different manufacturers approach the design of disc systems in different ways. The Amstrad approach has been to use an 'interface' along with the disc drive. The interface is the small box which plugs into the 'floppy disc' connector at the back of the computer. This unit contains 'firmware'; chips which hold some of the programs that are needed to control the action of the disc drive. Other parts of the control programs are held on the Master disc (the system disc) which comes along with the drive. The interface is, in fact, a miniature computer in its own right, complete with its own memory. The drive is linked to the Amstrad CPC464 by means of the data cable which is (permanently) attached to the interface. This terminates in two 34-way connectors at the far end, so that two disc drives can be attached. The manual that comes with your disc drive shows very clearly how these connectors are to be attached. When you buy a second disc drive you do not need another interface, and the second drive can be connected to the second connector of the existing cable.

The disc drive also comes with a mains cable to which no plug has been connected. Figure 1.1 is a reminder of how a suitable plug should be attached. You *must* be sure that a suitable fuse is fitted in the plug; a 3A fuse rather than the 13A one which usually comes with the plug. It's preferable to plug the disc unit into the same source of power as the computer, so a four-way socket strip, as illustrated in Figure 1.2 will be very useful to you. This

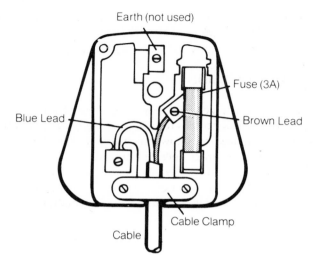

Earth (not used)

Fuse (3A)

Blue Lead

Brown Lead

Cable Clamp

Cable

Figure 1.1. Connecting the mains plug. Use a 3A fuse, not the 13A fuse that is supplied with the plug.

allows sockets for the CPC464, the disc drive, and a printer.

The controlling circuits for the disc system are contained mainly within the interface unit along with the disc filing system (DFS). A 'file' in this sense means any collection of data which can be stored on the disc. The DFS consists of a program, and most computers use a 'DOS disc' to hold this program. DOS is short for 'disc operating system. When this is done, a lot of the RAM memory (the memory that is free for you to use) is needed for holding the DFS. The Amstrad CPC464, however, uses chips within the interface to hold much of this information, which leaves most of the memory of the CPC464 free when you are using the normal AMSDOS system. Some memory has to be used, and this is also fitted to the disc drive

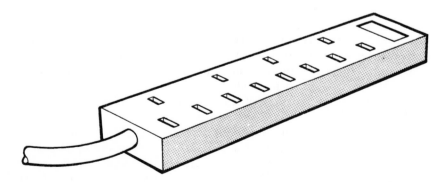

Figure 1.2. A four-way socket that allows you to operate a complete system from one wall-socket.

unit, so that only about 1.3K of the 41K of the CPC464 normally available to you for BASIC programs need be taken up when the disc system is used.

Tracks, sectors and density

The language of disc recording is very different from that of cassette recording. If your sole concern is to save and load programs in BASIC, you may possibly never need to know much about these terms. A working knowledge of how disc storage operates, however, is useful. To start with, it can clarify the reasons for the differences between using cassettes and discs. At a more advanced level, it can allow you to extract information from damaged discs, and to make changes to the information that is stored on discs.

Unlike tape, which is pulled in a straight line past a recording/replay head, a disc spins around its centre. When you insert a disc into a drive, the protective shutter is rotated so as to expose part of the disc. When the drive is activated a hub engages the central hole of the disc, clamps it, and starts to spin it at a speed of about 300 revolutions per minute. The disc itself is a circular flat piece of plastic which has been coated with magnetic material. It is enclosed in a hard plastic case to reduce the chances of damage to the surface. The hub part of the disc is also built up in plastic to avoid damage to the disc surface when it is gripped by the drive. The surface of each disc is smooth and flat, and any physical damage, such as a fingerprint or a scratch, can cause loss of recorded data. The jacket has slots and holes cut into it so that the disc drive can touch the disc at the correct places. The slot and one hole (one of each on each side) are covered by a metal shutter when the disc is withdrawn from the drive. You can see the disc surface if, holding the 'A' side uppermost, you insert your thumbnail into the slot at the right-hand side of the disc casing, near the front. By sliding your nail back, you engage the sliding peg which acts on the shutter, and you can turn the shutter until the disc surface is visible. Do *not* touch the disc surface, sneeze on it, or do anything which could leave any marks on the surface.

Through the slot that is cut in the casing (Figure 1.3), the head of the disc drive can touch the surface of the disc. This head is a tiny electromagnet, and it is used both for writing data and reading. When the head writes data, electrical signals through the coils of wire in the head cause changes of magnetism. These in turn magnetise the disc surface. When the head is used for reading, the changing magnetism of the disc as it turns causes electrical signals to be generated in the coils of wire. This recording and replaying action is very similar to that of a cassette recorder, with one important difference. Cassette recorders were never designed to record digital signals from computers, but the disc head is. Even the cassette mechanism of your CPC464 cannot cope really well with digital signals, because it is limited by having to use ordinary cassettes. The reliability of recording on a disc is

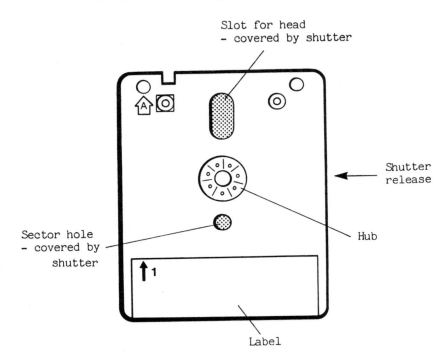

Figure 1.3. The slot in the casing of the disc is there to allow the head of the drive to touch the disc surface.

therefore very much better than you can ever hope for from a cassette.

Unlike the head of a cassette recorder, which does not move once it is in contact with the tape, the head of a disc drive moves quite a lot. If the head is held steady, the spinning disc will allow a circular strip of the magnetic material to be affected by the head. By moving the head in and out, to and from the centre of the disc, the drive can make contact with different circular strips of the disc. These strips are called 'tracks'. Unlike the groove of a conventional record, these are circular, not spiral, and they are not grooves cut into the disc. The track is invisible, just as the recording on a tape is invisible. What creates the tracks is the movement of the recording/replay head of the disc drive. A rather similar situation is the choice of twin-track or four-track on cassette tapes. The same tape can be recorded with two or four tracks depending on the heads that are used by the cassette recorder. There is nothing on the tape which guides the heads, or which indicates to you how many tracks exist.

The number of tracks therefore depends on your disc drives. The vast majority of disc drives for other machines use larger discs with either 40 or 80 tracks. Forty-track drives use 48 tracks per inch, and 80-track drives use 96 tracks per inch. The DDI-1 disc drive uses a 3-inch disc with 40 tracks, but with 96 tracks per inch. This forces you to find a source of these special discs, however, which are by no means common at the time of writing. In fact, at the time of writing these discs were in *very* short supply, and of the independent suppliers, only Disking were advertising them. Be very careful when you send for discs that you specify the 3-inch type. Several business computers, such as Apricot, have standardised on the Sony 3½-inch disc, and this size is quite easy to find. It is, however, *not* suitable for your DDI-1 disc drive.

Once you have accepted the idea of invisible tracks, it's not quite so difficult to accept also that each track can be divided up invisibly. The reason for this is organisation – the data is divided into 'blocks', or sectors, each of 512 bytes. A byte is the unit of computer data; it's the amount of memory that is needed for storing one character, for example. Each track of the disc is divided into a number of 'sectors', and each of these sectors can store 512 bytes. Conventional 40 or 80-track discs use ten sectors per track, but the DDI-1 system uses 9 sectors per track, allowing $512 \times 9 = 4608$ bytes to be recorded on each track. Two tracks are reserved on the Master disc (the *system* disc) for holding essential data, leaving 38 tracks for your use. This corresponds to a total of 175104 bytes free, which is 171K. It is possible to make use of the reserved tracks if you are, for example, storing only word processing text on a disc. In this way, 180K can then be stored on the disc.

The next thing that we have to consider is how the sectors are marked out. Once again, this is not a visible marking, but a magnetic one. The system is called 'soft-sectoring'. Each disc has a small hole punched into it at a distance of about 14 mm from the centre. There is a hole cut also through the disc jacket, so that when the shutter is swung aside and the disc is turned round, it possible to see right through the hole when it comes round. When the disc is held in the disc drive, and spun, this position can be detected using a beam of light. This is the 'marker', and the head can use this as a starting point, putting a signal on to the disc at this position and at eight others, equally spaced, so as to form sectors (Figure 1.4). This sector marking has to be carried out on each track of the disc, which is part of the operation that is called 'formatting'.

Formatting discs

Formatting discs, as we have seen, consists partly of the action of 'marking out' the sectors on a disc. The formatting action, however, should also test the disc. This is done by writing a pattern to each sector, and checking that an identical pattern is read back later. Failure to do so indicates a faulty sector, and a disc with such a fault should be returned to the supplier with a request for a replacement. These small discs cost three times as much as a conventional floppy disc, and they *ought* to be perfect. The prices will

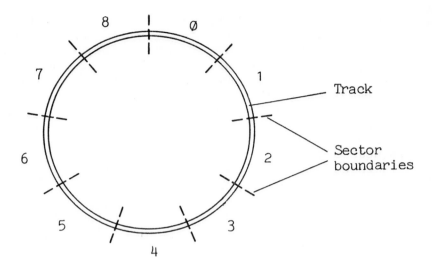

Figure 1.4. How the disc sectors are arranged. These are not visible, because they consist only of magnetic signals.

probably come down from their present levels, and some of the large suppliers are already quoting prices of around £39.90 for a box of ten.

Formatting, then, consists of marking out sectors and testing them. This takes about half a minute, and will normally end with a message which asks you if you want to format another disc. Any fault which is found at the formatting stage will be reported. This does not necessarily imply a *disc fault* however. All 3-inch discs make use of a small sliding shutter (Figure 1.5) which exposes or covers a hole at the front left-hand side of the disc casing. If

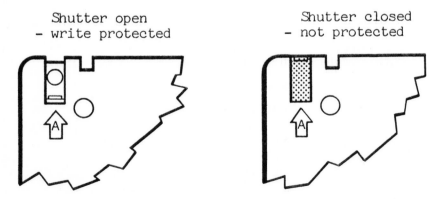

Figure 1.5. The write-protect hole and its shutter. You will need the tip of a ball-pen to slide this shutter in and out.

this hole is exposed, the disc is 'write-protected' which means that it cannot be formatted. Now if the disc is protected in this way, it's probably because you wanted to preserve some information that has been recorded on it. Since formatting will wipe the disc clean, the message is a warning to you that you might want to think again. If you really want to format, then you have to slip the plastic cover over the write-protect hole. Note that if you have been used to ordinary floppy discs of 5¼-inch size, that this protection action works in the *opposite* way. On the ordinary floppy, a slot has to be covered to protect the disc; on the 3-inch disc, the hole has to be *open* for protection.

The formatting action is carried out when a set of instructions has been typed and entered. The CPC464 disc system uses two controller programs, called AMSDOS and CP/M 2.2 respectively. Of the two, AMSDOS is intended for use with the Locomotive BASIC language of the CPC464, and it's the system that you will use along with programs that are written in BASIC. CP/M 2.2 is a more general disc system, which handles some of the tasks that are common to all disc operations, like formatting. In other words, if you want to format a new disc or reformat an old one, you have to make use of the CP/M operating system. First of all, you will need the Master disc. Make sure that the write-protect hole is exposed, because you cannot take risks with this disc – it is *valuable*. If you don't believe me, then just try getting a replacement! Insert the Master disc in the drive, making sure that it is the correct way round. The discs are double-sided, with the sides labelled as 'A' or 'B' at the front left-hand side, next to the write-protect hole. The actual recording and reading is carried out on the *under* side of the disc, but the labelling is placed so that side A or 1 is the one being used when this number is *uppermost*. The flap on the front of the drive unit is opened when you push the disc into the slot. Hold your Master disc with the 'A' side facing up. On the label of the Master disc, incidentally, side A is labelled as '1' and side B as '2', and this system is used on other labels. Slide the disc into the slot. Don't use any force to do this, because you can jam the disc if you do so. Press the disc in firmly until it stays put and clicks into place. The disc is now ready for formatting.

You then have to type the command which will allow the CP/M system to take control of the disc drive. This command is:

|CPM (or |cpm)

then press ENTER. As in Amstrad BASIC, commands can be in upper or lower case. To avoid confusion with other text, however, all command words will be printed in upper case in this book. We'll look later in more detail at the effect of this and similar commands. You will see the red 'drive working' light brighten, and hear the disc drive motor whirring. Soon the screen will clear to a bright pale-blue colour, change to 80-column mode, and display the message:

CP/M 2.2 Amstrad Consumer Electronics plc

followed on the next line by the prompt A> and the cursor. This distinctive screen layout is used to remind you that you are using CP/M and not AMSDOS. I, for one, find the letters hard to read in this format, and numbers *very* difficult to distinguish. If you find the same difficulty, then be particularly careful when you are using this mode.

You must now type the word 'format', and press ENTER. This will bring up the message:

Please insert the disc to be formatted into drive A
then press any key:

followed by the cursor. You must now remove the Master disc, and insert the disc which you want to format. Make sure that this disc is the correct way up for the side that you want to format (1 or 2 uppermost), and then press the spacebar or the ENTER key. Unless the disc is write-protected, you should then find that the formatting action takes place. If the disc is write-protected and you change your mind about formatting it, then press CTRL-C (CTRL key and C key together). This will abort the formatting program, and produce the message:

Please insert a CP/M system disc into drive A then press any key:-

You should then insert the Master disc, A side up, into the drive and press the spacebar or ENTER key. The drive will spin briefly, restoring the action of the main CP/M program. This same message will also appear if formatting has been successful, and you have answered 'N' to the question:

Do you want to format another disc (Y/N):

Finally, you will need to return to the Amstrad operating system if you want to make use of the disc with BASIC programs. With the Master disc in place, either side up, type AMSDOS (or amsdos) and press ENTER. This will restore the familiar screen with 40 characters per line, and the 'Amstrad BASIC 1.0' message.

The formatting action reserves some sectors on the third track of the disc. This portion is reserved as a way of storing information about the contents of the disc. To put it crudely, the disc system reads the first few sectors of this track to find if the filename for a program is stored on the disc, and then to find at which sector the program starts. With this information, the head can then be moved to the start of the program, and loading can begin. This part of the track is known as the directory, which keeps a record of what tracks and sectors have been used, and which are free for further use. The directory entries consist of filenames and numbers which indicate which track and sector is used for the start of each program or other file that is stored on the disc. The filename for a disc consists of up to eight letters for the main name, and (optionally) three letters for the 'extension'. It's easy to forget the limitation on filename length if you have been using cassettes for some time, because the cassette system allows filenames of up to sixteen characters. The 'extension' is also a novelty, and we'll deal with it later. To wipe a program or some data from the disc, simply remove its directory entry – the data remains stored on the disc until it is replaced by new data. This can *sometimes* allow you to recover a program that you thought you had erased.

Storage space

How much can you store on a disc? The Amstrad system uses 9 sectors on each track, and a maximum of 40 tracks; 38 tracks on discs which contain the CP/M system program. This makes a maximum of 360 sectors, if the system tracks are used as well. Of these, up to 4 sectors will be used for the directory entries, and this leaves 356 sectors free for you to use.

Each of these sectors will store 512 bytes, which is half of a kilobyte. If you take 356/2, giving 178, you end up with a figure of 178K on a single side of a 40 track drive. Not all of this will normally be usable, however, because data is not stored at every possible point on the disc. This is because the disc operating system works in complete sectors only. Suppose you have a program that is 1027 bytes long. The disc operating system will split this into groups of 512 bytes, because it can record 512 bytes on one sector. When you divide 1027 by 512, you get 2 and a fraction – but the DFS does not deal with fractions of a sector. Three sectors will be used, even though the last sector has only 3 of its 512 bytes recorded. When the next program is saved it will start at the next clear sector, so that the unused bytes are surrounded, and there is no simple way of making use of them. If you save many short programs on the disc you will find that a lot of space may be wasted in this way. A set of short BASIC programs, for example, will use one sector each. There is another way in which space can be wasted if you keep a large number of very short programs on a disc. Each program will have a separate directory entry, and when the directory track is full no more entries can be accepted. The system, however, allows up to 64 directory entries on a disc, so you would have to be very fond of short programs to run out of directory space!

The large amount of storage space, theoretically up to 180K, on a disc contrasts with the 41K or so which you have available for BASIC programs on the CPC464. For long programs, then, a disc system can be used as a form of extra memory. If a long program is split into sections, the sections can be recorded on a disc, and a master program entered into the computer. This master program can then call up different sections from the disc as needed, giving the impression that a very large program is, in fact, operating. The use of a disc system therefore allows you not only to load programs more quickly and store a lot of data, but also to use the computer as if it had a very much larger amount of memory.

Finally, Figure 1.6 lists some precautions on the care of discs. These may look rather restrictive, but remember that a disc is precious. It can contain a

Care of discs

1. Keep discs in their protective boxes when they are not inserted in the drive. If you drop a box, it will chip, but this is better than chipping the disc jacket.

2. Buy discs from a reputable source, such as Amsoft or one of the large disc suppliers. At these prices, you can't afford to take risks.

3. Never pull back the protective shutter unless you need to – which is normally never!

4. Never touch any part of the inner disc.

5. Keep your discs away from dust, liquids, smoke, heat and sunlight.

6. Avoid at all costs magnets and objects that contain magnets. These include electric motors, shavers, TV receivers and monitors, telephones, tape erasers, electric typewriters, and many other items which have surfaces that you might lay discs onto.

7. Label your discs well. If the label on the disc is not large enough, use self-adhesive labels in addition – but don't cover any of the shutters.

8. Remember that the disc is read and written from the *underside*.

Figure 1.6. Taking care of your discs. They are not as fragile as this might suggest, but remember that each disc can hold a lot of valuable programs.

lot of data, perhaps all of your programs. An accident to one disc, then, can wipe out all your work at the keyboard, or all the programs you have bought over the course of a year! Always make a backup copy, and always take good care of your discs. If you leave a fingerprint on a piece of tape, you may cause some loading difficulties on that piece of tape, but it's unlikely that you will lose a whole program. A fingerprint on the surface of a disc could make the directory impossible to read, so that the whole disc is useless. Similarly, a disc can be demagnetised by strong magnetic fields. These fields can be around loudspeakers, TV receivers or monitors, headphones, and electric motors. All of these should be regarded as potential disc-killers and avoided. Take very careful note of the advice in the DDI-1 Manual about siting the disc drive. You are told to avoid the left-hand side of the monitor, because this is where the magnetic fields are strongest. If you place your disc drive close to this side of the monitor, you may find that discs will not format correctly, and that you continually get error messages when you try to write or read discs. Even a small change of position may make a lot of difference, and it is a pity that the connecting cable between the interface and the disc drive is not longer so as to give you more scope for locating the drive in a good position.

Chapter Two
The Disc Filing System

What does the DFS do?

The disc filing system or DFS is, as we have seen, a program. This program is not written in BASIC, but in the form of direct commands in number-code to the microprocessor (the Z80) which operates the Amstrad CPC464. Code of this kind is called 'machine code'. If you want, or need, to know more about machine code, then I suggest that you turn to my book *Introducing Amstrad CPC464 Machine Code*, also published by Collins. The purpose of the DFS is to interpret the disc commands that you type, and convert these into signals that can be used to control the disc system and shift data to and from it.

Note that the name is disc *filing* system, not simply disc system. Filing implies the storage of data (such as string or number arrays) as well as BASIC or machine code programs. The DFS is therefore equipped to carry out the organisation of data which is needed to store it on disc and recover it later. That's something we'll come back to later in Chapter 5. Meantime we'll keep to the more straightforward uses of the DFS. Rather than looking at the commands of the DFS in alphabetical order, we'll look at them in the order that is most likely to be of use to you, starting with the use of discs for storing programs. First, however, we need to look at how the use of a DFS modifies the Amstrad CPC464 machine, and what problems this can create for you.

The first thing that you have to get used to is the order of switching on and off. When the disc system is switched on, it needs a short time to prepare for being used, and in this time it's important that it should receive no signals from the computer. It's equally important that there should be no disc in the drive. As you switch on the components of your system, then, you must always ensure that there is no disc in the drive, and that the disc drive is switched on *before* the computer. If you find that you have managed to reverse the order, then switch both off and start again. The method that I use is to keep the disc drive's own mains switch permanently on. When I switch off, I switch off at the computer and the monitor, then at the mains. This ensures that when I switch on, I switch the mains first, which will switch on the disc drive. I can then switch on the monitor and the computer, in that order. You will see on the front of the disc drive a pair of lights. The one next to the Amstrad name, at the lower part of the panel is green, and it simply indicates that the power is switched on to the drive unit. The red light above it and to the left is a 'busy' warning, and it will be on brightly while the disc unit is operating. While the disc unit is awaiting a command, this light is dim. You must *never* take a disc out of the drive or put another disc in while this light is fully on. A few programs as they operate will cause the red light to flash irregularly, but you will hear the drive whirring round as well, indicating that this is not an error. When you switch on the drive, you will see the green light come on, and the red light appears very dim. When you switch on the computer, the red light brightens slightly. You should *not* have any disc in the drive while you switch it on, because there is a chance of corrupting a disc if you do this.

Using your memory

Memory is one of the vital statistics of a computer, and it is organised in units that are called bytes. Each byte can store one character, but numbers are coded to make more efficient use of memory than having one byte allocated for each digit. The total amount of memory that the microprocessor of the machine can cope with in one lump is 65536 bytes. To distinguish one byte from another we number them, starting with 0 and going up to 65535 in our ordinary counting scale. Since 1024 bytes, in computing language, is 1K of memory, the Amstrad CPC464 is described as having 64K of memory, since $64 \times 1024 = 65536$. Most modern computers use this amount of memory, but the important quantity is how much of the memory is available for you to use. The CPC464 allows you to use almost 41K of the total of 64K for BASIC programs or for machine code.

An important difference which has been mentioned earlier, however, is that adding a disc system takes only 1284 bytes of memory from the computer. One manufacturer sells a 16K computer which has only 7K left when the disc system is added! Adding a disc system to your CPC464 leaves you with almost as much memory as you had before. This is a very great advantage, because it allows you to transfer programs from cassette form to disc form with less risk of running out of memory. The price that you pay for this convenience is that you can use only an Amstrad disc drive – the disc drives that you see at such tempting prices in the shops are for any other machine, but not Amstrad! You may, however, find that some suppliers will offer disc drives which have been modified to fit the CPC464. You should think twice before being tempted with bargain disc drives, however, because you may be cutting yourself off from a lot of useful software by having a non-standard system.

Loading and saving

We dealt with the formatting of a disc in the previous chapter. Once a disc has been formatted, you can use it for storage. The method that you follow for BASIC programs is very similar to the method used for cassette storage, and the form of the commands is almost identical. The most important difference is that you *must* use a filename for both LOAD and SAVE. You may have become accustomed to using LOAD" " with the cassette system to load the next program on a tape. If you use this command with the disc system, you will get the error message 'Bad command'. On a disc there is no 'next program', because all of the programs are obtained by finding a name in the directory, and then locating the correct sector. Similarly, a command such as SAVE" " is rejected. When you switch on a disc-equipped machine, the disc system is *automatically* switched in, so that all LOAD and SAVE commands refer to the disc system. If you want to make use of cassettes, you will have to signal this to the system.

If, for example, you have some BASIC programs on a cassette that you want to save on to a disc, then the procedure is as follows. Place the cassette that you want to use in the recorder. This should be a cassette whose program is not 'protected' in any way – if you understand machine code programming, you will know how to remove the protection from a program on cassette. Alternatively, you can buy one of the advertised 'unlocking' programs – they *do* work! Another option is to type and use the tape to disc utility program in Chapter 8 of this book. Place a formatted disc, with no write-protection, into the disc drive. Now if you simply used LOAD to try to get the program from tape, you would not succeed, because the effect of LOAD and SAVE are to make use of the disc system. You can, however, overrule this by using the command:

|TAPE.IN (ENTER)

first. This changes the coding in the computer so that you can LOAD from a cassette, but SAVE on the disc. You can then load in the program that you want to save. You will have to start by typing LOAD "NAME" (or just LOAD" " if you want the next program on the tape) and pressing ENTER. You will get the familiar message:

Press PLAY then any key:

and when you do this, the program will start to load. This action of loading from tape should present no problem other than the time it takes. Once the program has loaded, you may want to check it briefly by listing it or running it, just to make sure that it is the program which you want. Now type SAVE "MYPROG" using whatever filename you have decided to give the program. Remember that the disc system permits filenames of up to eight characters. You *must* use a filename when you load or save using discs. When you press ENTER, the disc drive will click, and almost immediately (unless it is a very long program) you will see the prompt reappear to indicate that the transfer is complete. Shortly after this, the red disc drive light will go out, and you will hear the disc motor stop. That's it! If you want to carry out the (unlikely) action of loading from disc and saving to tape, then you would use |TAPE.OUT instead of |TAPE.IN. The command |TAPE switches entirely to tape operation, both loading and saving, and |DISC switches back to 100% disc action. The presence of these DISC and TAPE.IN (and .OUT) commands makes it possible to carry out every conceivable transfer between tape and disc.

To load a program that is on disc, you can type LOAD "MYPROG" (or whatever filename you have chosen) and press the ENTER key. If the disc is correctly inserted in the drive, it will spin, and the 'Ready' prompt will reappear shortly to indicate that the program is loaded and ready. If you used the wrong filename, you will either get the wrong program or an error message, depending on whether a file of that name exists. If there is no program called MYPROG on the disc, for example, you will get the error message:

MYPROG . not found

Not all programs will load in this way. You will find, for example, that the ROINTIME demonstration program on the Master disc will not load in this way. That's because, like most games programs for the CPC464, it is written in protected machine code rather than in BASIC. A protected machine code program has to be RUN rather than just loaded, and if you try to use a LOAD command, you will get some form of error message. If, for example, you use LOAD"ROINTIME", you will get the 'not found' message. If you notice that the full title of the program is ROINTIME.DEM, and you use this filename, you will get the 'memory full' error message. You can make use of the program only by typing RUN "ROINTIME.DEM", and then ENTER. This loads and runs the program, but you will find that you need to press CTRL SHIFT ESC to leave the program. Once again, you can copy such programs only if you are reasonably proficient in machine code, or have purchased an unlocking program.

The ordinary LOAD command fails also to load the LOGO program which is on the B side of the Master disc. This is because LOGO is in machine code and has been saved by using CP/M. To load it, then, you must switch to CP/M, and because of the way that DR. LOGO has been recorded, this will also load the LOGO. Switch to CP/M by typing|CPM (ENTER), and wait. You will see the A> prompt, then the name LOGO and a copyright message. The more normal way of loading a CP/M program is to type |CPM, wait until the disc is ready, then type the name of the program, and then press ENTER. This is all that you need to load normally when CP/M is in use. Unless you use some of the (very expensive) business programs which have been transferred on to 3-inch discs, however, LOGO might be the only program that you are likely to load from CP/M!

Loading is generally much faster than storing, because the DFS carries out a check on data when it records, but not when it replays. If you get any sort of error message when you are saving a program, then it's wise to assume that the program has not been saved, and to save it again. When you have saved a program on disc, it's time to take a look at the way the disc keeps track of your program. This is done by reading the directory of the disc. Make sure that you are using AMSDOS (dark blue background, orange-yellow print), and then type CAT and press ENTER. If you happen to be using CP/M, then type DIR instead of CAT. The AMSDOS CAT command gives you a list, in alphabetical order, of the filenames, file types and size of each stored file. It also shows under this list how many kilobytes of storage remain unused and available on the disc. This is a more useful display than the one you get by using DIR in CP/M, because the DIR display does *not* show the file sizes, nor does it show the remaining space. On CP/M, however, you can find the size of a file by using STAT. Typing, for example, STAT ED.COM will produce the file size and arrangement on the disc of the file called ED.COM. When you use STAT, you have to follow it with the *full* filename, including the three letters which follow the dot.

You can also print out the DIR display, assuming that you have a printer connected. If you type DIR, and then follow it with CTRL P before pressing ENTER, the directory will be printed on paper as well as appearing on the screen. It's very convenient to keep printouts of your directories because you can then find what is on each disc without having to insert the disc and use CAT or DIR. With over one hundred discs in use, I wouldn't want to be without this facility!

Remember that each disc has two sides, but only one side can be read by a drive. You will have to turn the disc over to CAT or DIR the other side. If you have only one drive, the commands that we have looked at are all you need, but with two drives, you will have to select the drive that you want to use *before* you attempt to LOAD or SAVE or CAT that drive. The first drive is labelled 'A', and is the one which is attached to the connector at the *far* end of the cable. The cable has another connector, and the drive on this connector is labelled 'B'. At switch-on, drive A is always selected. If you want to select drive B, then type |B if you are using AMSDOS, or B: if you are using CP/M. In CP/M, you can add the drive letter to a filename. This means that you can be using drive A normally, but load a file called ADDFILE from drive B by using:

    B:ADDFILE

which will load this file from drive B, and then switch back to using drive A again. You should *not* attempt to use :B if you have only one drive, because this can cause the operating system to become jammed in a loop. To recover, press CTRL SHIFT and ESC together.

You *must* keep a careful record of the filenames that you use. This is because the disc drive will quite happily replace one program with another of the same name. If you have just completed a program and you want to save it, then always use CAT to read the directory to find if you have used a filename already. The old program is *not*, however, wiped from the disc. Instead, it is renamed with the extension label BAK. For example, suppose you wanted to save a BASIC program called "EFFORTS". If there is another BASIC program of this name on the disc, it will appear in the catalogue as EFFORTS .BAS – the extension name of BAS has been placed there *automatically* by the action of the system. When you record your new program using the same name, it gets the name of EFFORTS .BAS, and the other program is renamed EFFORTS .BAK. You can do this only once, though. If you save yet another program with the file name EFFORTS, then the first one will be wiped from the disc, the second one will be renamed EFFORTS .BAK, and the latest one will be labelled EFFORTS .BAS.

If you really want to prevent the replacing of a program, however, this can be done. For details, see the chapter on CP/M operations (Chapter 4). Though the protection is carried out by using CP/M, it is recognised by AMSDOS, and in a catalogue the filename is marked with an asterisk. Any attempt to save a file with the same name will then bring up an error message which shows the filename followed by the message 'is read only'. This rather cumbersome but useful protection should be applied to all valuable files. When you have a number of valuable files on a disc, you should write-protect the whole disc by flipping back the small shutter with the end of a ball-point pen or a nail-file. This will protect all of your files on that disc from being written over. It can't protect them from coffee or from stray magnetic fields, though!

Disc commands

Because the disc system for the CPC464 contains its own computing circuits, complete with some memory, many of the actions that we use to control the disc system have to be carried out by sending command words to the disc system itself. The words SAVE and LOAD are CPC464 command words, which operate on the cassette system if you have used |TAPE and forgotten to use |DISC later. There is another set of commands, however, which applies to the disc system only, and which has to be sent to the disc drive. These commands are all distinguished by the use of the '|' sign before the command name (like |TAPE and |DISC), and by the way that filenames can be included. Many of these commands are also available in slightly different form when you are using CP/M.

Retitling and erasing

As your use of discs increases, you may find that you want to group files that are related in some way on to one disc. It would then be very helpful if you could give this disc a title which would remind you of what it contains. This is possible on a number of other disc systems, but not alas on the AMSDOS. You can, however, delete and rename individual files and groups of files. The system for doing this is not exactly simple or straightforward compared, for example, with that of the BBC disc system, so a bit of practice with it will be useful.

Starting with deleting files, the keyword here is ERA (ERAse). You might think that this could be used in the form ERA "FILENAME", but it can't. Instead, you have to pass to the disc system the address in memory of where this name is placed. The BASIC of the CPC464 has provided for this by the command @. If you precede a variable name, number or string, with the @ sign, then the effect is to locate whereabouts in the memory that variable value is stored. For example, if you type X$="FILE" (ENTER) and then follow it with ?@X$, you will see a number (such as 374) appear on the screen. This is a memory address the number of the first of a set of bytes in memory that 'points to' the variable name. By 'points to', I mean that the contents of these bytes contain information on the length of a string and its location in memory. This is the way in which such information *must* be passed to the disc system when the | commands are used.

Suppose, for example, that we want to erase a file which is called ALLWORK. This has to be done in two steps. The first step is to assign "ALLWORK" to a variable name, such as X$. The second is to apply ERA to @X$. The two lines of commands are therefore:

    X$="ALLWORK" (ENTER)
    |ERA,@X$ (ENTER)

and the file will be erased from the directory after the second command has been executed. This is possible only if the file has not been protected. If the file has been made 'read only' by using the CP/M STAT command (see later), or if the whole disc is write-protected because of the write-protect shutter being pulled back, then the erasure cannot take place. If you want to erase a number of files which have very different names, then you can use a loop in BASIC which reads each filename from a DATA list, assigns each in turn to X$, and then carries out the ERA action.

ERA, however, is one of the many commands that can make use of the 'wildcard' character, *. The asterisk can be used to mean any collection of characters, so that if you assigned X$="E*", then this would mean *any name* which started with E. The asterisk can be used in various parts of a filename. For example, *.BAK would mean any 'old version' file, because it would refer to any filename followed by .BAK, like ERROR.BAK or PASSIT.BAK and so on. A 'name' such as *.* would mean *any* file. This wildcard system can be useful but you have to be careful with it, especially when you are erasing files.

Renaming a file makes use of the REN command. The form of the command is | REN,@N$,@X$, with the @ sign placed before each variable name. N$ in this case means the new name that you want to use, and X$ is the 'ex-name', the one you want to replace. Using X$ is preferable to using O$, because O and 0 are too easily confused. A renaming command needs three lines, with two assignments. For example:

```
N$="NEWFILE"  (ENTER)
X$="OLDFILE.BAS"  (ENTER)
|REN,@N$,@X$  (ENTER)
```

will rename the file that was called OLDFILE to the name NEWFILE. As usual, the disc must not be write-protected, and the name NEWFILE must not already exist on the disc. The *full name* of the old file, including extension, must be used in the assignment of the old string, X$. If this is not done, the change of name will not take place and you will get an error message such as:

OLDFILE . not found

to show that the extension was omitted. Putting a 'wildcard' into the old filename will cause a 'Bad command' error message. Because this command is so fussy about its syntax, you should always type it carefully and check each line before entering it. Remember that you won't have to repeat each part of the command if you want to try again. You will probably need to repeat only one of the assignments and the REN part if you have slipped up somewhere. If you want to rename a number of files, then set up a loop in BASIC, reading the old names and the new names from DATA lines.

Chapter Three
Digging Deeper

Hexadecimal codes

Unless you program in machine code, you probably haven't encountered the hexadecimal scale. If you use your disc system only as a convenient way of storing BASIC programs and data, and you have no intention of trying to read data from damaged discs or write machine code disc routines, altering CP/M routines, or transferring to disc programs from tapes which are copy-protected, then you can skip what follows, and reserve it for later. At some stage, however, you will probably want to make use of this information, and this is as good a place for it as any other.

Hexadecimal means scale of sixteen, and it's a way of writing numbers that is much better suited to the way the computer uses number codes. Our ordinary number scale is denary, scale of ten. This means that we count numbers up to nine, and the next higher number is shown as two digits, 10, meaning one ten and no units. Similarly, 123 means one hundred, two tens and three units. This counting scale, invented by the Arabs, replaced the Roman numbering system many centuries ago (except, oddly enough, for writing the dates of films and TV programs!). The unit of memory in the CPC464 and all other machines in its class is the byte, which can store a number between 0 and 255 (inclusive). A denary number for a byte may therefore be one figure (like 4) or two (like 17) or three (like 143). Hex (short for hexadecimal) is a much more convenient code for these numbers, and for address numbers. All single-byte numbers can be represented by just two hex digits, and any two-byte address by four hex digits.

One hex digit, then, can represent a number which, written in ordinary denary, can be between 0 and 15. Since we don't have symbols for digits higher than 9, we have to use the letters A,B,C,D,E, and F to supplement the digits 0 to 9 in the hex scale, as Figure 3.1 illustrates. The advantage of using hex is that we can see much better how address numbers are related. For example, consider the address for the start of BASIC in the ROM of the CPC464. This is the address which is used when you type RUN and press ENTER. In hex, this is 0170, whereas in ordinary denary numbers it is 368. Similarly, the address which is the start of the set used for screen memory is C000 in hex, 49152 in denary.

Denary	Hex	Denary	Hex
1	Ø1	9	Ø9
2	Ø2	1Ø	ØA
3	Ø3	11	ØB
4	Ø4	12	ØC
5	Ø5	13	ØD
6	Ø6	14	ØE
7	Ø7	15	ØF
8	Ø8	16	1Ø

Figure 3.1. How numbers 1 to 16 are written in hex.

The hex scale

The hexadecimal scale consists of sixteen digits, starting as always with 0 and going up in the usual way to 9. The next figure is not 10, however, because this would mean one sixteen and no units, and since we aren't provided with symbols for digits beyond 9, we use the letters A to F. The number that we write as 10 (ten) in denary is written as 0A in hex, eleven as 0B, twelve as 0C and so on up to fifteen, which is 0F. The zero doesn't have to be written, but programmers get into the habit of writing a data byte with two digits and an address with four even if fewer digits are needed. The number that follows 0F is 10, sixteen in denary, and the scale then repeats to 1F, thirty-one, which is followed by 20. The maximum size of byte, 255 in denary, is FF in hex. The maximum size of address in the memory of the computer, 65535, is hex FFFF. This is the number that we refer to as 64K. The K means 1024 in denary, #400 in hex. When we write hex numbers, it's usual to mark them in some way so that you don't confuse them with denary numbers. There's not much chance of confusing a number like 3E with a denary number, but a number like 26 might be hex or denary. The convention that is followed by machine code programmers of the Amstrad CPC464 is to mark a hex number with the hash sign (#) placed *before* the number. For example, the number #47 means hex 47, but plain 47 would mean denary forty-seven. The BASIC of the CPC464 will *not* recognise the use of # to mark a hex number, so you cannot enter numbers like #2B or #028A. It will, however, work with hex numbers if you prefix them with '&' or '&H'. The machine code program-writing pack, called DEVPAC, will require the use of the hashmark, and another such pack, the very popular ZEN assembler, needs hex numbers to be followed by the letter H, and will reject hash marks or ampersands (& signs). If you are using some types of utility programs that recover data from damaged discs, or which alter the machine operating system, you may have to enter numbers in hex. These utility programs usually contain routines for the conversion of numbers between hex and denary scales, so that you never need to carry out hex arithmetic for yourself. In addition, the CPC464 will carry out conversions for you. To find the equivalent of a denary number you use HEX$(number, digits). The 'number' is the denary number that you want to convert, and 'digits' means the number of hex digits that you want to use. This will normally be two for a byte and four for an address. For example, ?HEX$(210,2) will give the correct hex conversion to #D2, and ?HEX$(23540,4) will give the conversion to #5BF4.

Backing up

One feature of a disc storage system which is less pleasant is that an accident to a disc can result in the loss of a lot of information. If you break a cassette tape, it's possible to splice the tape, and with some juggling, lose only a part of one program. If you damage a disc, it's likely that all of the information on the disc will be lost as far as conventional LOAD commands are concerned. This does not mean that the information cannot be recovered from the disc, but this is a desperate measure, not to be undertaken lightly. It makes sense, then, if you have a disc full of valuable programs or data, to make a backup copy as soon as possible.

One sensible measure is to make a second copy of each program as you put in on disc. If you have bought programs on disc, however, you will need to make a backup copy, or two copies if the disc is a valuable one. The CPC464 system also allows you to copy the whole of a disc surface. Note that I mean *surface*, not disc. The discs are two-sided, and any backup method will copy only from one side. If you want to back up an entire disc, you will have to back up each side separately, turning the disc over at some stage so as to read from the other side. For many purposes, however, copying a file is enough, because you may only have one valuable program or data file on the disc. The operating system of the DDI-1 disc drive provides very well for copying a named file from one disc to another. If you use AMSDOS only, with programs in BASIC, this involves separate LOAD and SAVE steps. In other words, you will have to load the file into memory from one disc, and save it to another. This is straightforward enough when the files are BASIC programs, but the task is a lot more difficult when the files are machine code programs or data files. Fortunately, the utility programs which are part of the CP/M system are available for carrying out this essential task. We'll look at the CP/M FILECOPY backup utility later. A 'utility' is a program which aids you in some useful task like backing up a disc, printing what's on the screen, and so on.

Backing up is particularly easy when you have twin drives. With two drives in use, you can use a utility program to cause *everything* on one side of the disc in drive A to be copied to the disc in drive B, or the other way round.

The process is accompanied by a lot of clicking and whirring, as one disc is read and the other written, but at least you don't have to attend to the process. You can make yourself a cup of coffee while it is all happening. A low-cost alternative, if you have a lot of spare cassettes, is to keep backup copies on cassettes. Unless you are using business software, this is a more logical way to keep your backups, because the Amstrad cassette system is particularly reliable. For business software, however, it's much safer to backup on to another disc, and to keep this backup disc in a cool safe place well away from all the hazards to discs, such as loudspeakers, TV receivers, electric motors and anything else that uses magnets of any kind. Later in this book, we'll take a look at the sort of utility programs that are available for the CPC464.

Making backups

Of all the topics in disc use, that of making backup copies of individual files and of complete discs is the most important. The method which we have looked at so far, of loading into memory and saving on to disc, is simple enough for BASIC programs. It is, in fact, the only method that is available in the AMSDOS operating system. It can cater for machine code programs also providing that you know the essential information about the program. For example, if you have a machine code program from which you can break out into BASIC, then you can save this on disc. You need to know the address at which this program starts, and the length of the program in bytes. For example, suppose you have a machine code program which starts at address #03E8 (denary 1000) and which consists of 9060 bytes (denary). You can save this on disc by using:

SAVE"MCODE",B,1000,9060   (ENTER)

but this is no great help if you don't know where the start and end addresses happen to be. The CAT command applied to tape does not help you very much on this, because it does not give a display of the tape header. This is the part of the tape which carries the information about where the program resides in the memory. As it happens, the skilled machine code programmer has no problems in finding this information, and by the time this book appears, there will probably be a rash of programs on tape and on disc which will help you. In the meantime, however, Figure 3.2 shows a utility call HEADTST which will read the header of a tape program and print out the really useful information on it. This uses BASIC for most of its actions, but includes twelve bytes of machine code which will load the first 'header' section of a tape. This 'header' consists of 64 bytes which contain, in number coded form, all the information about the file that follows. Normally, this loads into the machine memory and is used without being accessible to you, the user, so that you never know what is on this header. The short piece of machine code which is contained in the BASIC program of Figure 3.2 will load the header part of the tape data into the memory, starting at memory address 2000 (denary). The BASIC part of the program can then extract information from the header simply by peeking into this part of the memory.

```
10 :TAPE: H=HIMEM: CLS:MEMORY 1980:M%=19
81
20 DEF FNGET(X%)=PEEK(X%)+256*PEEK(X%+1)
30 FOR N%=0 TO 11
40 READ D$:POKE M%+N%,VAL("&"+D$):NEXT
50 PRINT"Prepare cassette, press spaceba
r to start."
60 K$=INKEY$:IF K$=""THEN 60
70 CALL M%:M%=2000
80 PRINT:PRINT"Program ";
90 FOR N%=0 TO 15:PRINT CHR$(PEEK(M%+N%)
)::NEXT
100 PRINT:IF PEEK(M%+18)AND 1 THEN PRINT
"Protected" ELSE PRINT"Not protected"
110 PRINT"File type ";
120 X%=PEEK(M%+18)AND 14
130 IF X%=0 THEN PRINT"Coded BASIC"
140 IF X%=2 THEN PRINT"Machine code"
150 IF X%=6 THEN PRINT"ASCII characters"
160 IF X%=4 THEN PRINT"Screen image"
170 PRINT:PRINT"Start address is ";FNGET
(M%+21)
180 PRINT"Length is ";FNGET(M%+24)
190 PRINT"Execute address is ";FNGET(M%+
26)
200 DATA 21,D0,07,11,40,00,3E,2C,CD,A1,B
C,C9
210 MEMORY H::DISC
```

Figure 3.2. A utility which reads a tape header and prints the useful information.

How to use HEADTST

To use HEADTST, assuming that you have typed in the program and saved it on disc, load the program, and RUN it. The program allocates a chunk of memory for its own uses, and automatically switches the operating system to TAPE, rather than disc. If this is not done, then the program will attempt to read from the disc. This *can* be useful, but it's not what we want at the moment! You will get the usual message about pressing PLAY, then any key, at which you should make sure that your cassette is inserted and wound to the correct place. When you start the cassette, the header part only will be read. This is the part which sounds like a rapid change of note, and whenever it has been read the information will appear on the screen. The first line of information is on the filename. Remember that tape filenames can use up to 16 characters, so don't expect to be able to use the same filename when you save to disc. You will then see whether the tape is protected or not. A lot of machine code tapes are protected in some way, but not all in the way that is achieved by using SAVE with the P command. Others, however, use a BASIC 'loader' program which loads and calls the machine code, but with the machine code itself unprotected. The next information is on the file type, showing whether this is machine code or not. A 'coded BASIC' file means one that is a normal recording of a BASIC program, with each 'keyword' (such as PRINT or INKEY$) coded as a single byte. This is a direct copy of what is stored in memory when such a BASIC program is loaded, and it will normally be loaded back to the same memory location of 368 (denary). An ASCII file may be data that has been saved using PRINT#9, or it can be a BASIC program which has been saved using SAVE"name",A. Whichever it is, it consists of a set of ASCII codes which are easy to load and to copy. For a variety of reasons, this is a desirable form to save programs on disc, as we shall see later. The other possible file type, 'screen image', means a set of bytes which represents a picture on the screen, and has been obtained by saving the contents of the screen memory.

Following the file type, the program then prints out the start address. This is the address in the memory at which the first byte of the program is located. The length figure which follows then shows how many bytes of memory will be occupied. Finally, the execute address is a figure that is given only for a machine code program. This is the address at which the machine must start working on the program. The execute address is often the same as the start address for a machine code program. One very notable exception occurs when the machine code has been loaded by a 'BASIC loader'. In such a case, the execute address is often 0. This will cause the program to crash if RUN"" is used to start the program, because address 0 is the one which is used when the machine is switched on from cold. For this reason, it is called the 'cold-start' address.

How it works

The first line of the program clears the screen, switches to TAPE, and reserves memory. The effect of H = HIMEM is to save, as variable H, the value of the address that is used as the top of memory before the program runs. The top of memory is then shifted down to 1980. The effect of MEMORY 1980 is to ensure that no address higher than 1980 can be used by the BASIC program. This avoids corrupting the machine code, the bytes that are read from the tape, or the quantities that are stored near the top of the memory space for the disc system. Line 20 then defines a function FNGET, which calculates a number from a pair of bytes peeked in memory. Integer numbers are stored in memory as two bytes, with the lower byte storing values up to 255, and the higher byte storing the number of 256s. For example, the number 320 is 256+64, and would be stored as the two numbers 64 and 1, meaning 64+1*256. A number which is stored as 35 and 7 means 35+256*7=1827. The function needs the address of the lower byte, and will calculate the number from this information.

Lines 30 and 40 then read in and place into memory twelve bytes of instruction codes. These set up and call a routine in the ROM of the CPC464 which will read the header part of a tape and store its 64 bytes in addresses which begin at 2000 (denary). When this has been done, line 60 provides a 'press any key' step, and when a key has been pressed, the CALL M% in line 70 will make the machine code run. This will produce the usual cassette loading message on the screen, and when the PLAY key is pressed, the header of the tape is read. After this, M% is reassigned to 2000 so that the memory from this address can be peeked. Lines 80 and 90 get the filename (up to 16 characters) which will be stored at addresses 2000 to 2015. The next address of interest is 2018. If this is odd, then the program is protected, and the test in line 100 checks for this and prints the appropriate messages. The rest of this byte is also used to carry information about the type of file that follows the header. Figure 3.3 shows how this coding system operates, and why the action of line 120 can detect the codes. The results of this decoding are printed in lines 130 to 160.

The remaining actions consist of finding number values, using FNGET. The first important number is the start address. What is actually contained here is the address at which the bytes were originally stored when the program was recorded. The address which is passed to FNGET is 2021. Following this, at address 2024, the total length of the program is stored. Finally, from 2026, the execute address is read. These are the most important values to read from the header at this stage – you will find details of the other codes in the Amsoft publication *Amstrad CPC464 Concise Firmware Specification*. The program ends by restoring the original memory size, and the disc system. Unless the original memory boundary is reset, you will get a 'Memory full' error message when you try to SAVE a program after using this routine. Note that this program works only on the header of a tape; it does *not* load any of the bytes of the tape into memory. That's a topic that we'll deal with at a later stage, in Chapter 8.

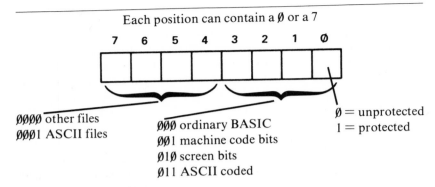

Example: If ØØØØØØØ1 appears this means ordinary BASIC, protected.

The action of AND 1 compares the byte No. 18 with ØØØØØØØ1, and gives the answer TRUE if *both* bytes contain a 1 in position Ø.

AND 14 compares the byte No. 18 with ØØØØ111Ø. This ignores bit Ø and gives:

ØØØØØØØØ for BASIC	(Ø in denary)
ØØØØØØ1Ø for m/c	(2 in denary)
ØØØØØ1ØØ for screen	(4 in denary)
ØØØØØ11Ø for ASCII	(6 in denary)

Figure 3.3. The coding system for byte No. 18 in the header, and how information is extracted from it.

Other backups

For backing up programs which are not BASIC, and about which nothing is known, we have to turn to the other operating system, CP/M. The CP/M package contains several utility programs which are stored on the CP/M Master disc, and the two which are of special interest to us at the moment are FILECOPY and DISCCOPY. You should by this time, have followed the instructions in the Amstrad DDI-1 Manual about making a backup copy of your Master disc. If you have not, then this is the time to do it! DISCCOPY is the utility that allows such a backup copy to be made, and we shall therefore look at it first. Before we do so, however, *you must make sure that the Master disc is write-protected.* This is to prevent any muddle. If you copy the contents of the Master disc on to a blank disc, all is well. If, by some terrible blunder, you copy the contents of the blank disc on to the Master disc, you will have lost the Master disc programs, and you will probably not have the use of the disc system until you can replace it. Such blunders are easy to make, especially in the wee sma' hours of the morning.

To copy the whole disc, as you would for a Master disc, insert the Master disc in the drive. The label should show side 1 uppermost, and you should then engage CP/M by typing|CPM. When you press ENTER, the disc will spin, and after a short time (when CP/M has been loaded) you will see the screen change to 80-character mode. This is when you have to be careful, because some numbers can be very hard to read in this mode, and a mistake can have unfortunate consequences. Fortuately, for the DISCCOPY program, no numbers have to be read. You simply type DISCCOPY and press ENTER. This is the universal CP/M method of loading a named program – just type the name and (ENTER). You will be asked to insert the source disc into drive A, and press any key. If you are copying the CP/M Master disc itself, you don't need to do anything at this point. If you are making a complete backup copy of any other disc, you should insert it now. It's a good idea to label your discs as 'SOURCE' and 'DESTINATION' before you start, so as to avoid confusion. This is less likely when you are copying the Master disc, but when you are backing up another disc, it may be less clear which is which. As long as you always write-protect the SOURCE disc, you are not likely to come to grief, but a lot of time can be saved by using clear labels. The DESTINATION disc need *not* have been formatted if you are using DISCCOPY, because DISCCOPY automatically carries out formatting as it operates.

Since a disc can hold much more data than will fit into the memory of the computer, the complete backup will involve reading data from the SOURCE disc, storing it in the memory, and then writing it to the DESTINATION disc. This has to be done five times in all to transfer all the data from the SOURCE to the DESTINATION. When each read is complete you will be prompted by a screen message to insert the DESTINATION disc into the drive, and press any key. As usual, it's best to press the spacebar or, if you have a slightly sticky spacebar, the ENTER key. After the last chunk of data has been read and written, the program repeats, asking if you want to copy another disc. If you do, you answer with the 'Y' key, and the process repeats. If you don't, then press the 'N' key, and you will be instructed to place the CP/M Master disc into the drive and press CTRL C. This replaces the DISCCOPY utility with the normal CP/M operating system again. Figure 3.4 shows the error messages that you might encounter while using this utility, and their causes. The alternative copying program, COPYDISC, can be used *only if you have two drives*. For this reason, it's often useful to make a backup copy of the Master disc that is *not* complete, but which contains only the utilities that are relevant to your own system. If you use COPYDISC in place of DISCCOPY (not a difficult mistake to make), you may find yourself wondering why it doesn't work, and how you can get out of it. Individual files are copied by using the other utility, FILECOPY.

Using FILECOPY

FILECOPY is a utility that allows files to be copied from one disc to another on a single drive. Unlike DISCCOPY, which was loaded simply by typing

'You must insert the source disc into drive A'

    No disc in the drive.

'You must insert a CP/M system disc into drive A'

    A system disc must be in the drive in order to return to CP/M.

'You must insert the destination disc into drive A'

    There has been no disc in the drive to receive the copy.

'The destination disc in drive A must be write-enabled'

    You have used a disc which has its write-protect shutter drawn back.

'**WARNING**: Failed to copy disc correctly. The destination disc should not be used until it is successfully copied onto'

    The program has been abandoned mid-way, and must be started again.

'The source disc has an unknown format'

    Disc cannot be read, program has been abandoned.

'Failed to read source disc correctly: track x sector y'

    Fault in the source disc at the named track/sector location. You *may* be able to correct this with a disc editor.

'Failed to write destination disc correctly: track x sector y'

    Bad sector(s) in destination disc, which should be replaced.

'Failed to read destination disc correctly: track x sector y'

    Faulty sector(s) or magnetic interference. Check position of disc drive and try again.

'Failed to verify destination disc correctly: track x sector y'

    As above.

'Failed to format destination disc correctly: track x'

    Disc fault or magnetic interference again.

'^C... aborted'

    You typed CTRL-C while the program was waiting for an instruction. Program abandoned.

Two other messages, 'Illegal message number' and 'Insufficient space' should not appear unless you have modified your CP/M system.

Figure 3.4. The error messages that you can encounter when using DISCCOPY.

the name, the name FILECOPY must be followed by information about the file that is to be copied. If, for example, you want to copy the program BOOTGEN.COM from the Master disc onto a spare disc, you will have to use the command FILECOPY BOOTGEN.COM (ENTER). FILECOPY, used by itself, is meaningless. The DESTINATION disc *must* be formatted.

    Though the FILECOPY command requires a filename, there is nothing to stop this from containing the 'wildcard' asterisk character. If, for example, you want to copy all the files which are CP/M utilities with the .COM extension, then you can use FILECOPY *.COM to do this. If you want to copy all files whose filenames start with B, then you can use

FILECOPY B* to copy these files. You can even copy all files by using
FILECOPY *.*, but this is rather pointless if the disc is fairly full, because it
would normally be easier just to use DISCCOPY for this job. Figure 3.5
shows the error messages that you can encounter when using FILECOPY.

'No SOURCE file present on input line'
> You did not type a filename.

'Syntax error in options'
> Incorrect user number.

'Failed to open SOURCE file correctly'
> File not found, or reading failure.

'Failed to close DESTINATION disc correctly'
> Usually means that disc directory is full, or disc fault.

'DESTINATION disc directory full'
> No room for file directory entry, start again with another disc.

'DESTINATION disc full'
> No storage space on disc, use another disc.

'The DESTINATION disc has an unknown format'
> Usually means an unformatted disc, or one formatted by a different make
> of computer. Can also mean a disc corrupted by a magnetic field.

'The SOURCE disc has an unknown format'
> Disc corrupted, or not an Amstrad disc.

'SOURCE disc missing'
> You didn't put it in! This can also mean that the disc is not *quite* fully
> home in the drive.

'DESTINATION disc missing'
> As above.

'DESTINATION disc is write protected'
> You forgot to slide the protection shutter forward, or have used the wrong
> disc side.

'Incorrect DESTINATION disc'
> You started copying the file with one destination disc and have changed to
> another.

'Failed to read SOURCE disc correctly'
> Possible disc failure, or incomplete file being read.

'Failed to write DESTINATION disc correctly'
> Failure of destination disc – try reformatting and start again.

'**WARNING**:DESTINATION file (name) is incomplete'
> The copy will not work because the file is not correctly closed. This is
> unusual.

'^C... aborted'
> You pressed CTRL-C when the program expected an input.

Figure 3.5. The error messages that you can encounter when using FILECOPY.

Chapter Four
The CP/M Operating System

So far, we have looked at the use of the AMSDOS operating system in more detail than the CP/M system. This is because anyone who programs the CPC464 in BASIC is more likely to use the AMSDOS system almost exclusively. CP/M is a system which is designed much more for the *user* of expensive business-biased software than the writer of programs in BASIC. It is a well-established system (first designed in 1973!), which is used mainly on computers which have no BASIC in ROM. When you use CP/M, *BASIC is switched out* so you cannot expect to load and run a BASIC program when you use CP/M. All of the programs which you use with CP/M will be in machine code, and unless you write machine code, or make use of a language (like Pascal) which can be compiled to machine code, you are unlikely to write programs using CP/M. In any case, the aids to machine code programming which are included with the CP/M package are designed for the old 8080 chip rather than for the Z80 which is used in your CPC464. This does not make these packages entirely useless, because 8080 code is compatible with Z80 code, but there are many better ways of writing true Z80 code. One of them is the DEVPAC set of two programs, available from Amsoft; another is the ZEN package, available from Kuma Computers. In this chapter, we shall look mainly at the commands of CP/M which do not require extensive knowledge of machine code. First of all, though, we need to look at the filename extensions. Remember that, although all the commands are shown here in upper-case (capital) letters for the sake of clarity, they can be typed in lower-case.

From using cassettes, you should be familiar with the idea of filenames. The main difference, if you use only AMSDOS, is that the filenames can have no more than eight characters. In addition to the main name, however, you are permitted an 'extension' of three characters following the main name. There *must* be a dot (period) between the main name and the extension. These extensions are necessary for CP/M, and so they are used in the AMSDOS system as well. Their purpose is to identify a file type correctly, and if you do not specify an extension for yourself, the operating system will supply one. The most common extensions are listed in Figure 4.1. This is a small selection, and if you use CP/M programs extensively,

.ASC	File of ASCII text.
.ASM	Assembly language program file.
.BAK	Backup file.
.BAS	BASIC program file.
.COM	CP/M transient program file.
.DAT	Data file.
.DOC	Document or text file.
.HEX	Machine code file.
.LIB	Library file.
.OBJ	Machine code (object code) file.
.PRN	Assembly language listing file.
.REL	Relocatable machine code file.
.SUB	SUBMIT file.
.TEX	Text file.
.TXT	Text file.
.$$$	Temporary file. Also used for an unreadable file.

Figure 4.1. Commonly used CP/M extension codes.

you could come across thirty or more of these extension names, all of which will be automatically assigned.

You can also assign extensions for yourself. Suppose, for example, that you are working on a program for yourself – we'll assume for the moment that it is a BASIC program, using AMSDOS. When you first try it out, you might want to save it under the filename of MYPROG.001, using the extension of 001 to mean that this is version 1. After some work on the program, you might want to save another version before running it, and this one could be saved as MYPROG.002. The use of the extension identifies this as a separate program, so that MYPROG:001 is not wiped out. When you save the final version of the program, you can type MYPROG as its filename, with *no* extension, and the system will automatically supply the extension of BAS, because this is a BASIC program. You can, of course, use these extensions as you please, but this use for numbering program versions is probably the most handy application. There are other extensions which can be used *preceding* the main filename, separated by a colon. The most important type of extension preceding a filename is the drive letter, A or B. You might, for example, have two programs, both called TESTIT.BAS but on different drives. One could then be called by typing A:TESTIT.BAS, the other by typing B:TESTIT.BAS, using the drive letters preceding the filename. These preceding letters are not likely to be of much interest to you if you are using only one drive, however. The other 'extension' at the front of a filename is the user number, which will be mentioned briefly later.

The CP/M commands

CP/M commands are of two types, built-in and transient. The difference is important. The built-in commands are contained in the ROM, and when you make use of them, you don't replace anything that is in the memory of the computer. The transient commands are carried out by loading a program (a 'command' file) into the memory and running it. This will replace anything else that happens to be in the memory at the time, so that you have to be rather careful about how you use these commands. In particular, you should not have a BASIC program in the memory and then switch to using a CP/M transient command unless you have a copy of the BASIC program on the disc. Since you will not normally use BASIC along with CP/M transient commands, this is not quite such a problem as it might seem.

We'll look at the transient commands of CP/M later in this chapter, but for the moment we'll concentrate on the built-in commands, which are listed in Figure 4.2. Each of these will be obeyed at once when its name (and any

---

DIR	Print directory.
TYPE	Print out named file.
ERA	Erase named file.
REN	Rename file.
SAVE	Save machine code in a block of memory.
n:	Select drive n.
USER	Enter user number.

Figure 4.2. Built-in commands of CP/M.

other data that is needed) is typed, followed by ENTER. Of these commands, you will by this time have used DIR to obtain the CP/M directory. You can obtain the same directory from AMSDOS by using |DIR, and rather more information from CAT. Staying with the CP/M DIR, however, you can also use this command to select directory entries. Suppose, for example, that you want a listing of all the BASIC programs on a disc. You can then type DIR*.BAS(ENTER), using the wildcard character to force the system to list any file which has the extension letters BAS. It is more likely, if you are working in CP/M, that you will require a list of the .COM files, or possibly .ASC or .DAT files. Once again, you can obtain these selective directories by using the asterisk wildcard character.

Of all the built-in commands, DIR is the one that you are likely to use most of all. If you have two drives, then you will find that you need to use A: and B: along with DIR. As you would expect, A: switches to drive A, and B: to drive B. If you use B: when you have only one drive connected (or if there is a connector fault in drive B), you will get the error message:

Retry, Ignore, or Cancel?

which requires you to press the R, I or C key. While the system is waiting for you to make up your mind, the disc keeps running. The appropriate response is to press the C key. You then find another error message:

Bdos Err On B: Select

A close study of CP/M manuals suggests that you should be able to get out of this one by pressing CTRL-C. I could *not* break out this way; the only way I could find of escaping from the endless loop of error messages was by using the CTRL-ESC-SHIFT set of keys. If you have only one drive, then, you should take care that you *never* use the B: command.

Using ERA and REN

By contrast with the rather clumsy way that AMSDOS uses the commands ERA (ERAse) and REN (REName), CP/M uses these built-in commands in a simple way. You must, however, be quite sure of what file, or files, you want to erase. The best method of proceeding is to use DIR first, and to copy the filename of the file that you want to delete. If there is no file of the name that you have typed, you will get the 'No file' message. Suppose, for example, that you want to delete MYPROG.001. If you type ERA MYPROG, you will find that this is *not* sufficient. You may get the curious error message 'Bdos Err On A:R/O' which normally means that the file is write-protected. In this particular case (unless the file really *is* write-protected), you need to start again by pressing ENTER (or any other key), then ERA MYPROG.001. When you specify the full filename with its extension, the erasure will be carried out.

You can use the wildcard character, *, but *not* to replace the whole of the extension. You can, for example use ERA *.BAS to erase all BASIC files, but you cannot specify ERA MYPROG.* to erase all files called MYPROG which might have different extensions. What you can use, however, is ERA MYPROG.00* to erase all versions of MYPROG from 001 to 009. If you get a 'Bdos Err' message in the course of using ERA, then press the spacebar or the ENTER key to get back to normal. It's very important to use DIR *after* an ERA command just to make sure that the erasure has been carried out as you wanted it.

The REN command works rather as the |REN command in AMSDOS does, but with straightforward filenames. The syntax of REN is:

REN NEWNAME.XXX=OLDNAME.XXX.

For example, if you have a file called REMS.BAS, you can rename it TEST.BAS by using REN TEST.BAS=REMS.BAS. If the file REMS.BAS is locked, then you will get the Bdos Err message 'File R/O' to indicate that the file is read-only, and its name cannot be changed until you have removed the write-protection. Unlike ERA, no wildcard characters are permitted *anywhere* in the REN filenames, because it would be ridiculous to rename a set of files to the same name. The error message which you get in this case is the filename reprinted on the screen with a question mark following it. Another error is to try to rename a file with a name that is already in use on the disc. This also will be refused, with the 'FILE EXISTS' message.

USER, SAVE and TYPE commands

The USER and SAVE commands are much less likely to be used by the CPC464 owner than the other CP/M built-in commands. USER is a way of identifying files which have been saved by one user of the system. The idea is useful when several users share a disc system, with each user having an identity number between 0 and 15. By typing USER 8, for example, you identify yourself as being entitled to load files which have been stored when this user code was in action. Since all the files on your disc have been stored using USER 0, there won't be any USER 8 files. If you type USER 8 (ENTER) and then DIR (ENTER), you will get the message 'NO FILE', meaning that there are no files with this USER number attached. Unless you are one of a set of disc users who write and save machine code files, this command is of little interest. If you want to keep your files secure, however, when strangers are around, typing USER 8 will prevent a DIR listing of the files. It might be useful when you are showing off the system on Club night! An alternative method is to use the number in the filename, as a pre-extension. For example, saving with the filename of 8A:MYPROG.BAS will alter the directory so that only user 8 will see this directory.

   SAVE is a peculiar and rather old-fashioned CP/M command which is useful only if you are saving blocks of machine code or text directly from CP/M. The CP/M SAVE action is quite unlike the normal BASIC SAVE action, and requires a different syntax – it is closer to the SAVE"Name",B action of Amstrad BASIC. The command was originally intended for machine code programmers, but nowadays, anyone who uses machine code will make use of an assembler program which will incorporate its own version of a SAVE command. So that you know something about it, however, here's how it's used.

   SAVE is used to write on to the disc any bytes that are stored in the 'transient program area', which means the memory addresses from #0100 (256 denary) upwards. A SAVE will *always* start at this address of #100, and you have to specify how much of the memory is to be saved. The amount is specified in units of #0100 (256 denary) bytes. If, for example, you need to save a short program of just a few bytes, the minimum you can SAVE is #0100 (256) bytes, which is one block or 'page'. You would therefore use SAVE 1 FILENAME.COM to save this under the name of FILENAME.

COM. No wildcards are permitted in this filename. Since you are most likely to use SAVE along with the transient program DDT, we'll take no further interest in it at the moment.

The TYPE command is one which is useful only for ASCII files. These might be BASIC programs which have been stored from AMSDOS by using the SAVE"Name",A command, or they might consist of data (names and addresses, for example?) which has been saved by using PRINT#9 in a database program. The reason for specifying ASCII files is that any other files are likely to cause odd effects. TYPE allows the contents of files to be displayed on the screen. Now if you send ASCII codes to the screen, you'll see normal characters appear, but codes in the range 0 to 31 can cause effects like turning off the cursor, setting a new MODE, clearing the screen and so on. Machine code programs are likely to contain such characters, and so are BASIC programs which have been saved in the normal way, without using the 'A' modifier. Try it for yourself – return to AMSDOS, and write a short BASIC program. Now save the program, using the filename "TESTXT",A. Return to CP/M, and type: TYPE TESTXT (ENTER). You will see your program appear on the screen. If you use TYPE on any other BASIC program which has been saved in the ordinary way, you will probably see a line of text, a few graphics symbols, and nothing else. You may find a mode change or other disturbing effects which may require you to 'reboot' (load CP/M all over again). The moral is to keep TYPE for ASCII files only. One of the utilities in Chapter 8 shows how to save the text that appears on the screen in such a way that it can be recovered by using TYPE.

The transient commands

As we saw earlier, a transient command is one which is kept stored as a file on disc, and it will be loaded and run only when called. All transient programs are stored in the memory of your CPC464 starting at address #0100 (denary 256), and will wipe out anything else which has been stored starting at this address. Figure 4.3 is a list of the commands which come under this heading. Of this list, you will probably have used DISCCOPY, FORMAT and FILECOPY already, and we'll look at some of the other transient programs in this section. Of these, STAT is probably the most important.

STAT, short for STATISTICS, exists to give you more information about files stored on a disc that you get from DIR. It can also be used to change the STATus of files, however, such as write-protecting, or removing write-protection. *You cannot use STAT unless there is a copy of STAT on your disc* as well as the files you want to examine with it. This means that STAT is one of the utilities that you may wish to copy on to other discs from the Master disc. If you have a set of files on a disc, but no STAT, you can usually transfer a copy of STAT, using FILECOPY, from the Master disc,

MOVCPM.COM	Configure a new CP/M system.
ED.COM	Edit assembly language files.
STAT.COM	Print information on files.
FILECOPY.COM	Copy file, single drive.
CHKDISC.COM	Check disc copy, needs two drives.
FORMAT.COM	Format new disc.
PIP.COM	Transfer data.
ASM.COM	Run 8080 assembler.
DUMP.COM	Show file content in hex.
SYSGEN.COM	Copy CP/M system to another disc.
DISCCOPY.COM	Copy complete disc using single drive.
SUBMIT.COM	Make a list of files run in succession.
DDT.COM	Monitor for 8080 machine code.
BOOTGEN.COM	Put CP/M tracks on program disc.
DISCCHK.COM	Checks that a copy is valid, single drive.
CLOAD.COM	Reads (unprotected) cassette file, transfers to disc.
CSAVE.COM	Reads from disc, transfers to cassette.
XSUB.COM	Places direct commands into a file.
LOAD.COM	Converts a .HEX file into a .COM file.
AMSDOS.COM	Returns to AMSDOS.
COPYDISC.COM	Copies disc, needs two drives.
SETUP.COM	Changes CP/M configuration.

Figure 4.3. The transient commands of CP/M.

or any copy of the Master disc. This is *not* always possible, however. If your disc has been used with AMSDOS only, and has no copy of the CP/M tracks (the system tracks) on it, then STAT cannot be loaded on to it. Similarly, if the disc is nearly full, there may be no room for STAT, which needs at least 6K of storage space. As so often happens, users of twin disc units have an advantage here. They can place the disc which contains STAT in drive A, and use the B: specifier for the filenames on a disc in drive B, so that STAT loads from drive A but works on files in drive B.

STAT has several varieties of syntax, some of which are useful even if you use mainly AMSDOS and BASIC. To start with, if you type STAT (ENTER) with no filename, you will get the statistics on the disc in drive A. These 'statistics' will be rather sparse; a reminder of the drive letter, an indication of protection, and the number of K of free space on the disc. The protection message will be R/O (read-only, meaning write-protected) or R/W, meaning no protection. When you use STAT in this way, the protection indication is meaningless, because a disc may be listed as R/O or R/W regardless of the position of its write-protection shutter. This is because STAT does not write on the disc, and the presence of the write-protect shutter is detected *only when the disc is written to*. Even the 'bytes free' number has to be regarded with some suspicion – I found that storing STAT on a disc did not alter the number that appeared here!

STAT really comes into its own when you apply it to individual files or groups of files. To apply STAT to a file, you follow STAT by a space, then type the filename with extension, and ENTER. For example, STAT TESTFIL.BASENTER will provide the statistics on the BASIC file called TESTFIL. These statistics will consist of the full filename, with the status (R/O or R/W) and a note of the number of records, bytes, and extent of the file. None of these figures will show you *exactly* how large a file is. The 'Recs' number shows the whole number of 128-byte units that the file uses. If the file consists of 129 bytes, for example, its Recs number will be 2. The Bytes number shows the whole number of Kilobytes assigned to the file. Once again, no fractions are shown, and a file of only 12 bytes will still produce a Bytes number of 1K. The Ext is an even less useful figure, which remains at 1 until the file is really long, more than 16K. We'll see later how we can find the exact size of a file, using the transient command DDT.

The use of STAT with filenames can take wildcards, such as STAT *.BAS which will give statistics on all BASIC files, and STAT G*.* which will give STATS on all files of any type which start with the letter G. You can also use STAT *.* which will give statistics on all files. Be careful to include the extension to the filename, even if it consists only of a wildcard. Note that a file will be shown as R/W in the 'Acc' (access attribute) column *unless* it has been protected. Using the write-protect shutter on the disc does *not* cause individual files to be shown as write-protected for the reason given earlier.

The most important use of STAT for our purposes is in altering the protection of files. This is done by following the filename with a space, and then a set of 'attribute' characters. These attribute chaiacters must start with the $ sign, and can then be R/O (read-only), R/W (read/write), DIR (appear in directory) or SYS (not in directory). For example, if you have a file called TRY.BAS, you can write-protect it by typing:

STAT TRY.BAS $R/O   (ENTER)

and if you have a file called REMS.BAS which is write-protected, you can release the protection by typing:

STAT REMS.BAS $R/W   (ENTER)

You can use STAT *.BAS to confirm that these alterations have been carried out. It can be very useful to have some files which do not appear in the directory, like the CP/M system file, and this can be done by using SYS. For example, a file called PRINTSET.BAS can be kept out of the directory by typing:

STAT PRINTSET. BAS $SYS   (ENTER)

and from then on it will be concealed from the user who types DIR. The file will *still appear* if STAT is used, so that, for example, typing STAT*.* will list this file with the others. It is marked out by having brackets around the filename. To restore a file like this to the directory, having found its name from STAT*.*, just type:

STAT PRINTSET.BAS $DIR   (ENTER)

which will restore the directory entry for this file. All of these varieties of the STAT command can make use of the wildcard characters in the filenames, so that a whole set of files can be write-protected or removed from the directory and so on. A less important use of STAT is to list 'device names'. These are the names that CP/M allocates to external devices such as the keyboard, screen, printer and so on. By typing STAT DEV: (ENTER), these can be listed. The listing is not of particular interest or use to you unless you are designing machine code programs for CP/M.

Other transient commands

When you look through the list of transient commands found by using DIR on the Master disc, it's rather discouraging to find how many of them are of little use to you. Another disappointment is to find how many useful-looking names conceal programs that are, in fact, only of specialist interest. In this section, we'll look at some of the other files on the Master disc, and comment on their usefulness or otherwise to the ordinary CPC464 user. Remember always that CP/M transient commands are designed for use with CP/M programs in machine code, and are of little or no interest if you program only in BASIC. Even if you make extensive use of CP/M programs, many of the transient programs are of little use to you.

Of the files that remain, PIP is one of the more useful-looking ones, but it is less useful than might appear. PIP is a general-purpose program which deals with transferring data, but most of the data transfers that you want to make are already covered by other commands. The most useful transfer, for example, is to send to the printer characters that normally go to the screen only. This is done simply, without using PIP, by pressing CTRL-P before starting the screen listing. Pressing CTRL-P again stops the process. This action, plus the FILECOPY and DISCCOPY programs, supersedes much of what PIP can do. You have to remember that CP/M is a very old system, designed for use by professionals, and incorporating features which are not quite so necessary on modern computers. In addition, because the system has grown over the years, PIP is a command which can take dozens of optional forms, some of which are useful, others not. The simplest syntax of PIP is:

PIP Destination=source

which will transfer data from destination to source. You have to specify what you want to use as destination and what you want to use as source. Both might be filenames, in which case PIP is being used to make a copy of a file under a new filename. This can sometimes be useful. A much more common use of PIP is with 'device' labels. A list of these is shown in Figure 4.4, and each has to end with a colon (:). Of the seven or so device labels that can be used in standard CP/M, the CPC464 system suggests four, of which CON: and LST: are the really useful pair. CON: can mean the keyboard when you are using this as source, or the screen if you are using it as destination. CON is short for console, another term from the dim past. LST means the listing device, in other words the printer. If you have no printer, many of the applications of PIP are rather pointless for you. Looking at a file on disc, for example, is more easily done by using TYPE, and the file copying actions are better performed by using FILECOPY.

CON: Entry and display device.
RDR: Receive information device.
PUN: Send information device.
LST: Print information device.
NUL: A source of 40 nul characters.
EOF: A source of end of file mark, CTRL-Z.
PRN: A printer output which formats copy.

Figure 4.4. A list of device names that can be used with PIP.

One useful function, however, is to join two files into one large file. This can be very useful if you keep program subroutines for attachment to a main program. If you program in BASIC, of course, this applies only to subroutines which have been saved using the 'A' option to create ASCII coded files. If, for example, you have a program MAIN.BAS and a subroutine set called SUBS1.BAS, then you can join them in a file called LARGE.BAS by using:

PIP LARGE.BAS=MAIN.BAS,SUBS1.BAS   (ENTER)

using the comma to separate the file names. You don't have to confine yourself to combining just two files in this way, because as long as you use the comma to separate the sections you can combine as many as you can type in one command; about a line and a half of typing. If you want to carry out several PIP actions, one after the other, you can use a rather different syntax of PIP. You can type PIP (ENTER), and this will load the PIP program and print an asterisk on the screen. You can then type a PIP command, such as NEW.BAS=OLD1.BAS,OLD2.BAS (ENTER), and this will be obeyed. After this has been done the asterisk will appear again, waiting for another command, but you don't have to type PIP again. When you have no more commands, typing (ENTER) by itself will return you to the normal CP/M commands.

The other uses of PIP are rather specialised. You *can* use PIP to accept text from the keyboard and store it in a file. This is done by using:

PIP WRITING:TXT=CON: (ENTER)

at which the disc finds the PIP program, then opens a file. The disc must not be write-protected – if it is, you will get the usual error message with the options of Retry, Ignore or Cancel, followed by the Bdos Err message (use CTRL-C to escape, with a Master or system disc in place). This is *not* a very useful method for entering text, however, because you have to learn a new set of keys. Instead of using the DEL key, for example, you have to use CTRL-H. After each use of (ENTER) to start a new line, you also need to use CTRL-J. The text is ended by using CTRL-Z. When you have such a piece of text, you can send it to the printer by using LST: or PRN:. LST: is noted in the DDI-1 Manual, but PRN: also works and is very useful. When, for example, you type:

PIP PRN:=WRITING.TXT (ENTER)

the text is sent to the printer, the lines are automatically numbered, and the output is broken up into pages of 60 lines. Any TAB characters in the text will cause the printer to leave an 8-column gap.

Any of the PIP commands can be modified by following them with optional extension letters. These letters *must be placed between square brackets*, and they can be selected from the set that is shown in Figure 4.5. Once again, this is rather specialised, but it can be turned to some advantage if you have a printer. For example, by using:

PIP LST:=CON:[FT8P60] (ENTER)

you can force the printer to type what you are typing on the screen. You have to press ENTER to get a line typed, and then press CTRL-J to get the line feed. You should *not* use CTRL-H to rub out a mistake, because the printer will take this as a signal to print. To rub out, you use the DEL key as usual, but what you see on the screen is a checker square for each DEL key use. This prevents the error character from reaching the printer, however, unlike CTRL-H. The F modifier prevents the printer from reeling out a whole sheet of paper before starting, and the T8 sets the tabulation stops to 8 columns. The P60 makes the printer take a new page after 60 lines.

PIP has a very wide variety of uses, as you can see from the lists and the few examples, but most of these applications are for the professional who is working with a much larger machine and with ASCII and machine code files. Most of the other transient programs are aimed at the machine code programmer, and detailed description would be pointless. Of these, though, DUMP.COM can be useful. The command DUMP must be followed by a full file name, and its effect is to display on the screen the contents of the file

Note: n means number needed, $ means string needed, ^ means CRTL key.

[B]	Block transfer. Was used in paper tape reading.
[Dn]	Delete any character after number n.
[E]	Echo characters to screen.
[F]	Filter out form feeds.
[Gn]	Copy from other user number n.
[H]	Hex format for paper tape.
[I]	Ignore nulls in paper tape inputs.
[L]	Convert upper-case to lower-case.
[N]	Add line numbers
[O]	Transfer machine code files, or non-ASCII files.
[Pn]	Put out form feed after line n.
[Q$^Z]	Copy file up to this string.
[R]	Copy system files.
[S$^Z]	Copy data starting with specified string.
[Tn]	Set tab stops every n characters.
[U]	Convert lower-case to upper-case.
[V]	Verify copy.
[W]	Copy to R/O file.
[Z]	Zero parity bit during transfer.

Figure 4.5. The extra commands of PIP which can be used within square brackets.

in *hex* codes. This is not something that would be useful to the BASIC programmer, and even the machine code programmer would normally prefer to have a disassembly. Nevertheless, for a quick check of a short machine code program, DUMP can be quite useful.

Other commands

Two commands of the CP/M transient set look rather familiar to anyone who has ever used Microsoft BASIC. These are CSAVE and CLOAD, and as the 'C' suggests, they are concerned with cassette use. There is a restriction, however, which prevents you from making use of these to transfer your programs from tape to disc. The restriction is that only ASCII coded tapes can be used. As it's unlikely that you'll have many ASCII coded programs, you might think that this provision is not really useful. You may, however, have a lot of data recorded on tape from data-gathering programs, such as a name/address file, a record of Football scores, the Golf Club membership list, and so on. This will be in ASCII codes, and so it can be used by CLOAD. CLOAD requires in the disc drive a system disc (with the

CP/M tracks put on by FORMAT) which has the CLOAD program in place, and which is not write-protected. You should know the filename for the tape, but if you do not, the program will load the first file it can find. As usual, the cassette messages will be suppressed if you place an exclamation mark as the first character of the cassette filename. The syntax for the command is:

CLOAD "tapefilename" discfilename (ENTER)

remembering that a tape filename can consist of up to 16 characters, but the disc filename cannot use more than 8 characters. If you don't put an extension on to the disc filename, none will be supplied by the system. If you don't provide a disc filename, the system will use up to 8 letters of the tape filename. The CLOAD command will not read protected programs, so you will have to use only unprotected tapes. In any case, if you want to transfer protected tapes to disc, it's better to make use of a utility that is specifically designed for the purpose. If you have one of the several tape utilities which allows you to make unprotected copies in ASCII format of protected tapes, however, this *could* be one way of getting your precious programs on to disc. The opposite program, CSAVE, allows ASCII files on disc to be transferred to tape. Since the price of 3-inch discs is three times as much as the price of the ordinary floppy disc, it makes sense to keep backups on tape rather than on another disc, but you have to remember that this applies to ASCII files only. You cannot use CSAVE to back up the really precious programs, which are the CP/M system and its utilities. Nevertheless, if you have large data files on disc and you want a cheap backup, then good-quality tape is not to be ignored, especially since the CPC464 tape system is so reliable. The only snag is that backup can take a long time. The syntax of the command is:

CSAVE discfile.ext,tapefilename

and, 1 can be added at the end if you want to use the higher speed save on tape. If you are using tape as a backup of a disc, you should ignore this provision and use only the lower speed, for which you don't need to specify anything. If you omit the cassette filename, then the system will use the same filename as was used for the disc file.

DISCCHK and CHKDISC

These utilities are for checking that a copy of a disc is an exact and perfect copy. CHKDISC is for use with twin drives only – you put a disc in drive A and its copy in drive B, then use CHKDISC to compare the discs, byte by byte. DISCCHK does the same more slowly, and will instruct you when to insert the source disc and when to insert the copy disc. If you find, incidentally, that for some reason these utilities refuse to load even when you have spelled the name correctly for the fourth time, then try loading another utility, such as DISCCOPY, and then aborting by pressing CTRL-C when the program runs. You should find then that normal action is restored. The cause is probably corruption of some of the CP/M operating system in the low RAM memory of the CPC464.

DDT, ED and ASM

These three are specialised programs for machine code programmers. Because some of the commands make use of the instruction set of the old 8080 chip, they are likely to have little appeal for programmers of today. DDT is a 'debugging' utility for machine code, a monitor as it would now be called. It is called into action by typing DDT (ENTER) or DDT filename (ENTER), depending whether you want to use it to search through itself or another file. The main sub-commands of DDT are shown in Figure 4.6 – the

---

Note: DDT uses hex numbers. s means start address, e means end address, b means breakpoint address, d means destination address, c means constant byte, name means filename.

As	Assemble from address s.
Ds,e	Display memory from address s to address e.
Fs,e,c	Fill memory from s to e with constant c.
Gs,b	Start program running at s, break at b. More than one breakpoint can be used.
Iname	Insert filename.
Ls,e	List disassembled code from s to e.
Ms,e,d	Move block of memory from s to e so as to start at d.
Ra	Read file to address.
Ss	Read and alter memory starting at s.
Tn	Trace n steps of the program.
Un	Execute n steps, no trace.
Xx	Examine and alter Z80 state. The 'x' refers to register code letters.

Figure 4.6. The main commands of the DDT utility. These are of interest mainly to machine code programmers.

most interesting ones are D and L. **L** allows a disassembled listing, and can be followed by a start number and end number, both in hex. The disassembly is, however, in 8080 code, and not everyone remembers it nowadays! The **D** command gives a hex dump, but with the added refinement of a set of columns of ASCII characters that correspond to any codes in the correct range. This allows you to read copyright notices, error messages and other items which might not otherwise come to your attention. The DDT program extends from address #0100 to #13A0, and any program that you load in with DDT (by having its filename following DDT), will be loaded in from this address onwards. When you make use of this additional load, the last address that is used will be displayed on the screen as well as the 0100 starting address. As you might expect by now, all addresses are in hex. Note that you can write in assembly language by using the 'A' option of DDT. The snag, as usual, is that this uses 8080 assembly language only, and there is no direct provision for saving. For writing 8080 assembly language, the ED utility is rather more useful. Once ED has been used to write assembly language, ASM can be used to assemble it into machine code, and record a file of this code. This file can then be converted into a .COM file by the LOAD command. If it looks very tedious, you're right, it is. If you are serious about writing in machine code, it makes more sense to use a good modern Z80 assembler, save the machine code with the extension .HEX, and then use LOAD to convert into a COM file.

Chapter Five
BASIC Filing Techniques

What is a file

I have used the word 'file' many times in the course of this book to mean a collection of information which we can record on a disc. Programs in BASIC are one type of file, and the only type, incidentally, which permits the use of LOAD and SAVE in a straightforward way, with no 'modifying' letters like A, B or P. As you will know by now, the best type of file for BASIC programs is the ASCII file, since this is the one which can be used both by AMSDOS and by CP/M routines. In this chapter, however, I shall use the word 'file' in a narrower sense. I'll take it to mean a collection of data that is *separate* from a program. For example, if you have a program that deals with your household accounts, you would need a file of items and money amounts. This file is the result of the data-gathering action of the program, and it preserves these amounts for the next time that you use the program. Taking another example, suppose you devised a program which was intended to keep a note of your collection of vintage 78 rpm recordings. The program would require you to enter lots of information about these recordings, such as title, artists, catalogue number, recording company, date of recording, date of issue and so on. This information is a file, and at some stage in the program, you would have to record this file. Why? Because when you load a BASIC program and RUN it, it starts from scratch. All the information that you fed into it the last time you used it will have gone – unless you recorded that information separately. This is the topic that we're dealing with in this chapter; recording the information that a program uses. The shorter word is 'filing' the information. In this chapter, we are dealing with filing programs that are in BASIC, so we shall not make any use of CP/M.

Knowing the names

You can't discuss filing without coming across some words which are always used in connection with filing. The most important of these are 'record' and 'field'. A *record* is a set of facts about one item in the file. For example, if you have a file about vintage steam locomotives, one of your records might be used for each locomotive type. Within that record, you might have wheel formation, designer's name, firebox area, working steam pressure, tractive force... and anything else that's relevant. Each of these items is a *field*, an item of the group that makes up a record. Your record might, for example, be the SCOTT class 4-4-0 locomotives. Every different bit of information about the SCOTT class is a field, the whole set of fields is a record, and the SCOTT class is just one record in a file that will include the Gresley Pacifics, the 4-6-0 general purpose locos, and so on. Take another example, the file 'British motorbikes'. In this file, BSA is one record, AJS is another, Norton is another. In each record, you will have fields. These might be capacity, number of cylinders, bore and stroke, gear ratios, suspension system, top speed, acceleration... and whatever else you want to take note of. Filing is fun – if you like arranging things in the right order. The importance of filing is that all of the information can be recovered very quickly, and that it can be arranged in any order, or picked out as you choose. If you have a file on British motorbikes, for example, it's easy to get a list of machines in order of cylinder capacity, or in order of power output, or any other order you like. You can also ask for a list of all machines under 250 cc, which ones used four-speed gearboxes, which were vertical twins. Rearranging lists and picking out items is something which is much less easy when the information exists only on paper.

Disc filing

In this book, because we are dealing with the CPC464 disc system, we'll ignore filing methods that are based on DATA lines in a BASIC program, or on the use of cassettes. Though you may be experienced at filing with cassette systems, I'll explain filing from scratch in this chapter. If it's all familiar to you, please bear with me until I come to something that you haven't met before.

To start with, there are two types of files that we can use with a disc system; serial files, and random access files. The differences are simple, but very important ones. A serial (or *sequential*) file places all the information on a disc in the order in which the information is received, just as it would be placed on a cassette. If you want to get at one item, you have to read all of the items from the beginning of the file into the computer, and then select. There is no way in which you can command the system to read just one record or one field. More important, with cassette files you can't change any part of a record, or add more records in the middle of such a file. Files of this type on disc are much more useful, because records can be read and checked much more quickly, but adding or changing items still presents problems. A random access file does what its name suggests – it allows you to **get** from the disc one selected record or field without reading every other one from the start of the file. You might imagine that, faced with this choice, no-one would want to use anything but random access files. It's not so simple as that, though, because the convenience of random access filing has to be paid for by more complication. For one thing, because random access filing allows you to write data at any part of the disc, it would be very easy to wipe out valuable data, or even the directory, with a program that was badly designed.

We'll start, then, by looking at serial files, which are also easy to record on cassette. All of the AMSDOS commands for serial filing are identical to the commands of the cassette filing system. This makes the change very easy if you have been using filing on cassette and you then upgrade to disc. If you have never used cassette files, of course, it's all new.

Serial filing on disc

We'll start by supposing that we have a file to record, called CAMERAS. On this file we have records (such as Nikon, Pentax, Canon, Yashica and so on). For each record we have fields like Model, Film size, Shutter speed range, Aperture range (standard lens), Manual or Automatic, and so on. How do we write these records? First of all, we need to arrange the program that has created the records so that it can output them in some order. The usual procedure will be to take the records in some chosen order, and output the fields of the record in some order as well. Figure 5.1 for example, shows

```
100 RC$="":X%=0:DIM Field$(5)
110 CLS:PRINT TAB(15)"DATA ENTRY":PRINT:
PRINT"Type X to end entry.":PRINT
120 INPUT "Record name - ";RC$: IF RC$="X
" OR RC$="x" THEN 190
130 REM NEED TO RECORD THIS ON DISC
140 X%=X%+1:FOR N%=1 TO 5
150 PRINT"Field item ";N%;" ";:INPUT Fie
ld$(N%)
160 REM NEED TO RECORD THIS ALSO
170 NEXT N%
180 GOTO 120
190 REM END OF FILE
200 PRINT"There are ";X%;" records on th
e file."
```

Figure 5.1. How to organise data for disc writing. The example uses five fields in a record.

how we might arrange this part of a BASIC program so as to input a number of records, with five fields to each record. The number of fields is five, so the fields are input from the keyboard using a FOR N%=1 TO 5 loop. The number of records isn't fixed, so we use a GOTO loop, which keeps putting out records until it finds one called "X" or "x", which is the terminator. I haven't used a WHILE...WEND loop, because this forces you to enter a lot of dummy field information in the last record. Note that we haven't used an array for holding these items, because an array has to be dimensioned, and we don't know in advance how many items we will have. Instead of storing the items in an array for future use, they will be recorded on disc. The points where the disc recording routine would be fitted are shown in the REM lines 130 and 160. Each item, field or record, is treated as a string. This is because strings are easier to work with – you will not, for example, get any error messages at the INPUT stage because of a mismatch of variable type. The other good reason for using strings is that a string is a set of ASCII characters, and these files are *always* recorded as ASCII files.

That deals with the organisation of the data for putting on to disc, but how do we actually put it on the disc? There are several stages, and the first one is to open up the 'data channel', which is assigned with the number 9. This means assigning a filename which will be recorded on the disc, and sending data to the disc with the PRINT#9 command. The 9 is a number code that the machine will use to distinguish the disc drive from the screen windows or the printer. Each time you want to make use of a file, then, you must have a filename, and this has to be used to prepare for recording on the disc by using the OPENOUT command.

The purpose of using the filename and the channel number 9 is to organise data. The disc stores all data in units of 512 bytes. It wouldn't make sense to spin the disc and find a place on the disc just to record one byte at a time, so when you record or read a disc, it's always one complete sector, or as much of a sector as possible, at a time. In fact, the operating system of the CPC464 uses 2K blocks of data, which would fill four sectors. Some of the memory of the CPC464 has to be used to hold data which is being gathered up for recording, or which is being replayed. The channel number 9 is an identifying number for the piece of memory that is being used, so that the machine finds the correct data in the correct part of the memory. Using this channel number avoids the need for you to have to allocate parts of the memory to use in this way as buffers. The memory which is used for this purpose lies at the top of the usable range. To see this in action, switch on from cold, and type ?HIMEM. On my machine, this gave the number 42619. If you now type OPENOUT "test" (ENTER), and then ?HIMEM, you will see that the number is now 38523. The difference is 4096, equal to 4K, or two buffers each of 2K. If you now type CLOSEOUT(ENTER), you will see that ?HIMEM gives the original figure of 42619 again. HIMEM means the top of usable memory, and it is shifted down when files are to be read or written, and restored at the end of filing commands.

Opening the file

After that short diversion, back to our filing program. Before we start to gather the data together for filing, we need to 'open a channel' for the data. This is done using the OPENOUT command. OPENOUT has to be followed by a filename, and if you have used cassette files previously you will have to remember that disc files must use no more than eight characters. In addition, it helps if you can give the filename some useful extension label. The 'standard' extension for data is .DAT, so it makes sense to use this unless you have some pressing reason for using something else. You can, of course, use numbers like .001, .002 and so on, to show different batches of data by the different extensions, or you can include these numbers in the main name, as, for example, CAMERA01.DAT. To take another example, the line:

OPENOUT "AIRCRAFT.DAT"

prepares to write a file called AIRCRAFT. When this line is executed, the disc will spin for a short time, preparing for the file, *but the filename will not appear on the directory/catalogue* because no data has been put into the file. The buffer space will also be prepared in the memory. As always, you can place the drive letter ahead of a colon if you have more than one drive.

The use of the OPENOUT command opens a file – which means that we can make use of the file for writing data on to the disc. It also means that the disc is prepared for the file. Any file that exists on the disc already and has the same name of AIRCRAFT will *not* prevent you from opening this file. This means that you have to be rather careful about how you use files, because one file will wipe out another of the same name. This, however, makes it very easy to update and modify files, as we shall see. If you want to lock a file you will have to make use of the CP/M STAT command *after* your BASIC data filing program has ended.

Printing to the file

It's at this stage that we need to make use of the loops in the writing program. Within these loops, we need to have a line something like:

160 PRINT#9,Field$(N%)

PRINT#9 means put the information out on channel 9, the channel for the disc system, so that PRINT#9 will *eventually* put out to the disc system the data that follows. In this example, it's Field$(N%). N% is the number in the FOR...NEXT loop, so that as the loop goes round, we will put on to the disc Field(1), then Field(2), then Field(3)... and so on. We also need to write the record name, and this is done within the loop, by using a line such as:

130 PRINT#9,RC$

without using an array (because of the unknown amount of dimensioning). Figure 5.2 shows an example of a very short and simple program of this type which has been adapted from the first example. You can enter anything you like into this, but it makes more sense to enter something that you can easily check. Since the file is called AIRCRAFT, you could make each record name an aircraft type, and each field some feature of the aircraft, like wingspan, engine details, number of crew, and so on. You can, of course, easily change this program so that it has another title that suits the information that you might want to use.

```
10 OPENOUT "AIRCRAFT.DAT"
100 RC$="":X%=0:DIM Field$(5)
110 CLS:PRINT TAB(15)"DATA ENTRY":PRINT:
PRINT"Type X to end entry.":PRINT
120 INPUT "Record name - ";RC$:IF RC$="X
" OR RC$="x" THEN 190
130 PRINT#9,RC$
140 X%=X%+1:FOR N%=1 TO 5
150 PRINT"Field item ";N%;" ";:INPUT Fie
ld$(N%)
160 PRINT #9,Field$(N%)
170 NEXT N%
180 GOTO 120
190 REM END OF FILE
200 PRINT"There are ";X%;" records on th
e file."
210 CLOSEOUT
```

Figure 5.2. A program which writes to a serial file.

Before we move on, consider what this program has done. It has created a file called AIRCRAFT.DAT, and allocated a channel number of 9 to this file. It has then stored the data as it came along, in the sequence of RECORD, then FIELDS. Finally, the file has been recorded and closed by using CLOSEOUT. This last step is *very* important. For one thing, you don't actually record on the disc *any of the information* in this short program until the CLOSEOUT statement is executed. That's because it would be a very time-consuming business to record each item of a file at a time. What the DFS does, remember, is to gather the data together in memory. This is the 'buffer' piece of memory, placed just above HIMEM, and it will be written to the disc only under one of two possible circumstances. One is that the buffer is full, so that there are four sectors full of data (2048 bytes) to write. The other is that there is a CLOSEOUT type of statement in the program. For a large amount of data, the disc will spin and write data each time the buffer is full. The CLOSEOUT command then writes the last piece of data, the one which doesn't fill the buffer. It also writes a special code number, called the end-of-file code (EOF). This can be used when the file is read, as we'll see later. If you forget the CLOSEOUT statement, you'll leave the buffer unwritten, with no EOF – and cause a lot of problems both in your programs and possibly with your disc system. Forgetting the CLOSEOUT is called leaving your files open, and you wouldn't like to be seen like that, would you?

The biggest danger is when you are testing a program. If there is an error, such as a syntax error, which stops the program from running, there will be no CLOSEOUT carried out, and the files will be open. If you had typed a lot of data, you would lose it if you then went on to correct the program and run it again. The correct procedure is to close all of the open channels. In this example, it's easy – you only have to type CLOSEOUT and press ENTER. For a large program you would probably find it better to write an ON ERROR GOTO line which, when an error ocurrs, closes files and ends . This automatically ensures that files are never left open. The CLOSEOUT ensures that your data will be recorded.

When you use an INPUT statement to gather up the data, you can find that with a lot of data you will hear the disc start and stop at intervals. That's an indication of the buffer transferring data to the disc. You can't use the keyboard while the transfer is taking place, but the time that's needed to write a sector is fairly short. You will find that the keyboard cannot be used during this time. In this example, there is nothing like enough data to fill a buffer. You will hear the disc spin when the OPENOUT command is executed, and again when the CLOSEOUT command is executed, but not at any time between these two unless you enter a huge amount of data.

Getting your own back

Having created a file on disc, we need to prove that it has actually happened by reading back the file. A program which reads a file must contain, early on, a command which opens the file for reading. This is OPENIN, and it must use the same filename as was used to write the file. If we recorded a file using the name 'AIRCRAFT', then we must not expect to be able to read it if we use 'CAMERAS' – or any other name. Misspelling can haunt you here! Once the channel has been opened, we can read data with INPUT#9, which will be followed by the variable name that we want to assign to each item. This command reads an item from the disc, and will allocate it to a variable name for printing the item or other use, according to what we have programmed. The number of reads can be controlled by a FOR...NEXT loop if the number is known, or it can make use of the EOF marker if the number is unknown. By testing for EOF, then, we can make the program stop reading the file at the correct place.

The example of Figure 5.3 shows both methods in use. The number of

```
100 DIM FX(5)
110 OPENIN "AIRCRAFT.DAT"
120 WHILE EOF=0:CLS:PRINT TAB(12)"AIRCRA
FT DETAILS":INPUT#9,Name$
130 PRINT"Type is ";Name$:RESTORE
140 FOR N%=1 TO 5
150 INPUT#9,Gen$(N%)
160 READ Field$:PRINT Field$;" ";Gen$(N%
)
170 NEXT
180 PRINT"Press spacebar for next record
"
190 K$=INKEY$:IF K$=""THEN 190
200 WEND
210 CLOSEIN:PRINT"END":END
220 DATA Wingspan,Length,Crew No.,Engine
s,Range
```

Figure 5.3. A program which reads the serial file.

fields has been five, so that a FOR...NEXT loop can be used to control the input of the fields. The number of records, however, has not been settled by a FOR...NEXT loop, so we have to keep reading the file until the EOF byte is found. This is done in line 120 by testing EOF in a WHILE...WEND loop. If EOF is not zero, then the file is closed, and the program ends. As you can see, this has been put into the WHILE...WEND loop, because EOF needs to be tested *before* another item is read. If you read again from a file like this, you will get the 'EOF Found' error message, and the program will stop. Unless you have arranged for an ON ERROR GOTO line to close files for you, the files will still be open. Leaving a reading file open is not quite such a disaster as leaving a writing file open, but it's still very undesirable. Note that the disc does *not* spin each time you press a key to get another record. This is because a complete sector or set of four sectors is read each time, and if the information that you want is all in one buffer load, the disc need not be used. Sorry if I seem to be labouring this point, but a newcomer to discs sometimes finds it difficult to remember.

Now this simple example shows a lot about serial filing that you need to know. When you use discs, then, the name that is used with OPEN (IN or OUT) is the filename for the file on the disc. Any other file that is later recorded with the same name will not overwrite this file, because the old file changes to a .BAK file. The system therefore provides for easy file replacement, *and* for reasonably good file security. This is an important point to emphasise if you have been using cassettes, because you have more control over where a file is recorded on a cassette. You can write a file called

INDEX at the start of a tape, for example, then wind the tape on slightly and record another, different, file with the same name. You certainly can't record two files with *identical* names on one disc. Even if the files have the same main name, the older one will have the extension .BAK to distinguish it. In addition, a file is closed by writing the EOF character. How, then, can you update a file, particularly if you want to add more items to the end of the file?

Updating the file

There are two answers, if we stick to serial filing. One possibility, which is the simplest one for short files, is to load the whole file into the memory of the computer, make the alterations (your BASIC program will have to be written so as to provide for this), and then write the file again, wiping out the earlier version. The other possibility is to open two files, one for reading and the other for writing. You don't need to have dual disc drives for this, though it makes life much simpler if you do. This means that the computer will maintain two buffers. You read one record from the reading file and you can, if you wish, display it. If it's all right, it's then written (to the buffer initially). If the record has to be modified, you can do so. If extra records have to be added, this is equally simple. Each time a buffer empties, the disc will spin and a read or write will take place. This 'simultaneous' operation is possible because of the use of different OPEN commands, which control different buffers. In practice, it's a matter of writing your program to suit.

Figure 5.4 shows a simple program which allows you to extend the file that was created by the program of Figure 5.3. Note, however, that the files use *the same* names, even though I have assumed that both files will be on the same disc. This is because the OPENOUT file and the OPENIN file are treated separately, using different buffers. This saves any problems of deleting the old file and changing the name of the newly created file. The operating system will see to it that the new file is recorded as AIRCRAFT.DAT, and the old file is renamed AIRCRAFT.BAK. One point we have to be *very* careful about, however, is closing files. The CLOSEIN command is used whenever the program has finished reading the old file, and the CLOSEOUT command is used whenever the last of the new files has been added.

Looking at the program in detail, line 110 opens two files *with the same names*. One, however, is an input file, and the other is an output file. The input file will be used by INPUT#9, and the output file by PRINT#9, so there should be no conflict between them, since they use separate buffers. Line 120 clears the screen and issues a PLEASE WAIT notice. If your files are long, it may take the disc some time to do all the reading and writing, and this notice is a reminder that it's all happening. Never leave a user with a blank screen, even if the user is always yourself! In these lines 120 to 150,

```
100 X%=0
110 OPENIN "AIRCRAFT.DAT":OPENOUT"AIRCRA
FT.DAT"
120 CLS:LOCATE 14,11:PRINT"PLEASE WAIT":
WHILE EOF=0:INPUT#9,Name$:PRINT#9,Name$
130 FOR N%=1 TO 5
140 INPUT#9,Gen$:PRINT#9,Gen$
150 NEXT N%:WEND:CLOSEIN
160 CLS:PRINT TAB(15)"ADDITIONS":PRINT:P
RINT
170 INPUT"Aircraft name ";Name$:IF Name$
="X" OR Name$="x"THEN 220
180 X%=X%+1:PRINT#9,Name$:FOR N%=1 TO 5
190 PRINT"Field item ";N%;" is ";:INPUT
GEN$
200 PRINT #9,Gen$:NEXT N%
210 GOTO 170
220 PRINT:PRINT"You have added ";X%;" it
ems."
230 CLOSEOUT
240 PRINT"END":END
```

Figure 5.4. Extending a serial file by reading, and rewriting.

data will be read in from the old file and written out to the new one until the EOF marker is found. When this happens, the WEND in line 150 takes effect, and the next command is CLOSEIN, which shuts down the reading file. The writing file is still open, however, with its buffer containing data that has been read so far. You can now add more data, using the same lines as you used in the program of Figure 5.2. When an X or x is typed in response to the request for a record name, then the program displays the number of added items, closes the write file (so recording the file), and stops. Quite easy, really, but in this program, no provision has been made for altering any of the records that are read from the old file. This is a routine which we can easily add – and that's the next thing to look at.

Changing a record

It's not difficult to find how to alter a record on a file. You read the item, print it, and then change the item before rerecording the file. The main problem is finding a neat way of doing this. The program of Figure 5.5 shows one approach which I use in my own file programs. This is to read the whole of one record, display it on the screen, and give the user the chance to edit or leave as need be. The editing is visual, rather than by the old-

```
100 DIM Gen$(5):X%=0
110 OPENIN "AIRCRAFT.DAT":OPENOUT"AIRCRA
FT.DAT"
120 CLS:LOCATE 14,11:PRINT"PLEASE WAIT":
WHILE EOF=0:INPUT#9,Gen$(0)
130 FOR N%=1 TO 5
140 INPUT#9,Gen$(N%)
150 NEXT N%:GOSUB 1000
160 FOR N%=0 TO 5:PRINT#9,Gen$(N%):NEXT
170 WEND:CLS:LOCATE 14,11:PRINT"PLEASE W
AIT":CLOSEIN:CLOSEOUT
180 PRINT"END.":END
1000 CLS
1005 LOCATE 1,23:PRINT"Press arrow key t
o move cursor, space   to alter item, CO
PY to end edit."
1010 PX%=5:PY%=4
1030 FOR N%=0 TO 5
1040 LOCATE PX%,PY%+N%
1050 PRINT Gen$(N%):NEXT
1060 PX%=1:PY%=4
1070 LOCATE PX%,PY%
1080 PRINT">";:FOR J=1 TO 100:NEXT
1090 LOCATE PX%,PY%
1100 PRINT" ";:FOR J=1 TO 50:NEXT
1110 IF INKEY(47)=0 THEN GOSUB 2000
1115 IF INKEY(9)=0 THEN RETURN
1120 IF INKEY(0)=0 THEN PY%=PY%-1
1130 IF INKEY(2)=0 THEN PY%=PY%+1
1140 IF PY%<4 THEN PY%=9
1150 IF PY%>9 THEN PY%=4
1160 GOTO 1070
2000 CALL &BB03:PX%=5:LOCATE PX%,PY%:PRI
NT SPC(34);
2010 LOCATE PX%,PY%:INPUT;Gen$(PY%-4)
2020 PX%=1:RETURN
```

Figure 5.5. A file editing program which uses a visual menu choice.

fashioned method of numbering the entries and asking for a number to be entered. When the record is displayed, a flashing arrowhead points at the first field. If you want to leave the record as it is, then press the COPY key, and this will bring up the next record. If you *do* want to change a record, move the arrowhead to the record using the cursor-up and cursor-down keys, the arrowed keys above and below the COPY key. When the arrowhead points to the field that you want to change, press the spacebar. This wipes out the field name on the screen, but not in the memory. You can now type a new field name or number, and terminate it with the ENTER key. Only when you have pressed the ENTER key is this new field entered, and if you want to change your mind, you can delete your entry and type the old entry again. When a change has been made in this way, the arrowhead still points to the same field, and you can make another change to this or, by shifting the arrowhead, to any other field. When you have finished editing the record, you can press the COPY key to bring up the next record. The process will continue for as long as there are records to read. The amended file will be recorded as AIRCRAFT.DAT, and the old file will be renamed AIRCRAFT.BAK. Note, however, that the visual editing system is useful only if the fields are short – a field which spreads over more than one line will cause problems.

How it works

Lines 100 to 140 follow the pattern which should be familiar to you by now. The files are opened, one for reading and the other for writing, and the WHILE EOF=0 loop will load in each record until the end of the file. The record name is assigned to Gen$(0), however, to make it easier to work with the fields in one array. The new items start with the GOSUB 1000 in line 150. This carries out the editing, and when editing of a record is complete, this subroutine will return. The amended or unamended record is then put into the new file by line 160, and the WEND in line 170 brings up the next record.

   In the subroutine, the screen is cleared, and a message about the editing commands is printed at the bottom of the screen. Lines 1010 to 1050 then print the record name and each field on to the screen. Note that this works only if each field is of less than 35 characters, because the whole method depends on using one line for each entry. In line 1060, X and Y positions for the cursor are assigned to PX% and PY%, and a loop starts in line 1070. In the loop, the '>' character is printed at the cursor position, held for a short time, then removed. Four keys are then tested by using the INKEY command. INKEY(47) tests the SPACEBAR, and if this is pressed, the GOSUB 2000 calls up the replacement routine. INKEY(9) tests for the COPY key, and causes a return from the subroutine if this key is pressed. The other two tests are for the cursor movement keys, and if one of these keys is pressed, then the value of PY% is altered. Lines 1140 and 1150 then test the value of PY%, to ensure that it does not stray outside the line limits, and line 1160 completes the loop.

   When the SPACEBAR is pressed, the first action in line 2000 is CALL &BB03. This is a machine code call to the operating system, and its effect is to remove any codes from the keyboard buffer. This is essential, because when any key is pressed, its code is stored in memory until it is read. When the cursor movement keys are used, their codes accumulate in this keyboard buffer despite the fact that the program is using the keys differently. As a result, when the program leaves the loop, these codes are read and acted on. For example, if you have used the down-cursor key twice to shift to the second field, there will be two 'shift down' codes in the buffer. There will also be a 'space' code because you pressed the SPACEBAR. The effect would be to make the '?' prompt for the INPUT stage appear at the line you have selected, but the cursor would appear two lines down and one space across. This can be avoided if the buffer is emptied before the INPUT step, and this is done by the CALL &BB03. If you are curious about this and other calls to the operating system, they are documented in an Amsoft publication, the *Concise Firmware Specification*.

With the buffer flushed out like this, the PX% number is changed so as to locate the first character of the entry, and the SPC(34) clears most of the line. The next LOCATE instruction places the cursor back at the start of the field name, and the INPUT then allows you to make the change. By using Gen$(PX%−4), you assign the new entry to its correct place in the array. Line 2020 then restores the value of PX% to place the arrowhead correctly, and the routine returns. The effect is quite impressive, though the key actions in the loop are slightly 'sticky' because of the time delays. If longer fields are used, it would be possible to modify the routine to make use of, say, two lines per field. In any case, this and the previous routine demonstrate how serial filing can be used with advantage on a disc system. In many cases, you will find this type of filing more useful than random access filing, which is never easy with any disc system.

Chapter Six
A Database Example – Filing Cabinet

This chapter consists mainly of one long listing (Figure 6.1) for a database type of program. The program is called Filing Cabinet, and it allows you to specify four heading titles for the fields of your records. These field names are recorded on the disc, and will be used from then on. They might, for example, be Name, Address, Age, Telephone Number. You can then enter information, add, delete or change information, read all of the data or select items as you please. These are the normal actions of a simple database. Looking at the length of the program, you might wonder how long a complicated program would be, but this *is* a simple version. There is no facility, for example, for printing records of any field in alphabetical order. This is, you see, a skeleton database, which has been included to illustrate the use of the DDI-1 disc drive for this type of program. Once you have this program up and running, *and have completed reading this book*, you should be able to add whatever extra trimmings you need.

```
10 OPENOUT"DUMMY":MEMTOP=HIMEM
20 MEMORY HIMEM-1:CLOSEOUT
30 ON ERROR GOTO 1420:ON BREAK GOSUB 280
40 NL$=CHR$(10)+CHR$(13)
50 REM FILING CABINET by Ian Sinclair 19
85
60 DIM H$(4),E$(4)
70 M$="Please make sure that the disc is
   in"+CHR$(10)+CHR$(13)+"the drive, corre
ct way up."
80 J%=1:Y$="Please answer Y or N.":Z$="P
ress any key..."
90 RESTORE:FOR N%=1 TO 4:READ H$(N%):NEX
T
100 REM Place in lines 60 to 80 any prin
ter setup instructions that you need.
110 REM
120 REM
```

Figure 6.1. The database program, "FILING CABINET".

```
130 DATA First,Second,Third,Fourth
140 CLS:T$="Filing Cabinet":GOSUB 290
150 T%=2:GOSUB 1430:PRINT:PRINT"Do you n
eed instructions? ";Y$
160 GOSUB 300:IF K$="Y"OR K$="y" THEN GO
SUB 310
170 CLS:T$="MENU":GOSUB 290
180 PRINT:PRINT "1.Start NEW type of fil
e.":PRINT"2.Start ENTRY in file.":PRINT"
3.DELETE,CHANGE or ADD items.":PRINT"4.L
IST complete file.":PRINT"5.PICK one ite
m.":PRINT"6.END Program."
190 PRINT:PRINT"Please choose by number.
":GOSUB 300:K%=VAL(K$)
200 IF K%<1 OR K%>6 THEN PRINT"1 TO 6 ON
LY- PLEASE TRY AGAIN.":GOTO 190
210 IF K%=1 THEN GOSUB 440:GOTO 260
220 K%=K%-1:IF F$=""THEN GOSUB 1390
230 GOSUB 1300
240 ON K% GOSUB 540,650,690,790,1050
250 GOSUB 1310
260 CLS:PRINT"Do you want to return to t
he menu?"
270 PRINT:GOSUB 300:IF k$="Y" OR K$="y"
THEN 180
280 CLOSEIN:CLOSEOUT:MEMORY MEMTOP:PRINT
"END.":END
290 PRINT TAB(20-(LEN(T$))/2);T$:RETURN
300 K$=INKEY$:IF K$=""THEN 300 ELSE RETU
RN
310 CLS:T$="INSTRUCTIONS":GOSUB 290:PRIN
T
320 PRINT TAB(2)"This program allows you
 to set up and":PRINT"use a serial file
database. You will":PRINT"be asked to pr
ovide four titles, which"
330 PRINT"will be recorded along with a
filename.":PRINT" You can then use the o
ther options to":PRINT"put entries into
the file, with your":PRINT"headings appe
aring as prompts. You can"
340 PRINT"add to the file, change or del
ete items":PRINT" and list the file as y
ou wish."
```

Figure 6.1. contd.

```
350 PRINT:PRINT"The main restriction is
that you must":PRINT"NOT enter anything
which contains a":PRINT"comma. You need
Menu Item 1 only when":PRINT"you start a
 new file for the first"
360 PRINT"time. For the rest of the time
 that":PRINT"this file is in use, the ot
her options":PRINT"apply. Keep one disc
side for each":PRINT"different file- you
 can keep a copy of":PRINT"this program
on each disc side as well."
370 PRINT
380 PRINT M$
390 PRINT:PRINT Z$
400 GOSUB 300
410 RETURN
420 INPUT Q$:IF LEN(Q$)>38 THEN PRINT"To
o long- please change now.":GOTO 420
430 RETURN
440 CLS:T$="New File Specification":GOSU
B 290:T%=2:GOSUB 1430
450 PRINT:PRINT"Now select your four tit
les for this":PRINT"new file, using ENTE
R after each title.":PRINT"Only four tit
les can be used.":PRINT
460 FOR N%=1 TO 4:PRINT H$(N%);" is- ";:
GOSUB 420:PRINT Q$
470 E$(N%)=Q$:NEXT
480 PRINT"End of titles specification- n
ow we ":PRINT"need a filename of up to e
ight ":PRINT"characters- no more.":PRINT
490 INPUT"Filename is- ",F$
500 IF LEN(F$)>8 THEN PRINT"Too long- ei
ght characters only.":PRINT"Please try a
gain.":GOTO 490
510 F$=F$+".DAT":E$(0)=F$
520 OPENOUT"HEADS.DAT":FOR N%=0 TO 4:WRI
TE#9,E$(N%):NEXT:CLOSEOUT
530 RETURN
540 CLS:T$="Entry of Items.":GOSUB 290:T
%=2:GOSUB 1430
550 PRINT"Items can now be entered until
 you ":PRINT"enter X as the first of a s
et."
```

Figure 6.1. contd.

```
560 PRINT"Entry No. ";J%
570 PRINT E$(1):INPUT Q$:IF Q$="X" OR Q$
="x"THEN 630
580 PRINT E$(2):INPUT R$
590 PRINT E$(3):INPUT S$
600 PRINT E$(4):INPUT U$
610 WRITE#9,Q$:WRITE#9,R$,S$,U$
620 J%=J%+1:GOTO 560
630 J%=J%-1:PRINT"End of entry.":T%=2:GO
SUB 1430
640 RETURN
650 CLS:PRINT:PRINT"Do you want to - ":P
RINT:PRINT"1. ADD to the file.":PRINT"2.
 CHANGE an item.":PRINT"3. DELETE an ite
m.":PRINT"4. RETURN to the main menu."
660 PRINT:PRINT"Please select by number.
":GOSUB 300:K%=VAL(K$):IF K%<1 OR K%>4 T
HEN PRINT"1 to 4 only- please try again.
":GOTO 660
670 ON K% GOSUB 1070,1110,1210,1290
680 RETURN
690 CLS:T$="FILE LISTING":GOSUB 290:T%=2
:GOSUB 1430
700 PRINT:PRINT"Do you want to use the s
creen or the":PRINT"printer for your lis
ting?"
710 PRINT:PRINT"Please press P or S key.
"
720 GOSUB 300:IF K$<>"P"AND K$<>"p"AND K
$<>"S"AND K$<>"s" THEN PRINT"P or S only
 - please try again.":GOTO 720
730 Z%=0:IF K$="P" OR K$="p" THEN Z%=8
740 C%=1:WHILE NOT EOF: GOSUB 1320
750 PRINT#Z%,"Item ";C%;"_"
760 GOSUB 1330:PRINT#Z%,E$(1);": ";Q$+NL
$+E$(2)+": ";R$+NL$+E$(3);": ";S$+NL$+E$
(4);": ";U$+NL$
770 C%=C%+1:IF Z%=0 THEN PRINT Z$:GOSUB
300
780 WEND:RETURN
790 PRINT:T$="PICK AN ITEM":GOSUB 290
800 PRINT:PRINT"You can pick by number (
N) or by ":PRINT"letter (L)."
```

Figure 6.1. contd.

```
810 PRINT:PRINT"Please press N or L key
now."
820 GOSUB 300:IF K$<>"N" AND K$<> "n" AN
D K$<>"L" AND K$<> "l" THEN PRINT"N or L
 only _ please try again.":GOTO 820
830 IF K$="N" OR K$="n" THEN GOSUB 860
840 IF K$="L"OR K$="l" THEN GOSUB 940
850 RETURN
860 PRINT"What number item do you want?"
:PRINT"Type number, then press ENTER key
."
870 INPUT X%:N%=1
880 WHILE NOT EOF:GOSUB 1320
890 GOSUB 1330:IF N%=X% THEN CLS:PRINT E
$(1);": ";Q$+NL$+E$(2);": ";R$+NL$+E$(3)
;": ";S$+NL$+E$(4);": ";U$:GOTO 920
900 N%=N%+1:WEND
910 PRINT"Item not found"
920 T%=1:GOSUB 1430:PRINT:PRINT"Press an
y key to return.":GOSUB 300
930 RETURN
940 CLS
950 PRINT:PRINT"Type first few letters o
y key to return.":GOSUB 300
930 RETURN
940 CLS
950 PRINT:PRINT"Type first few letters o
f the first ":PRINT"entry. Don't forget
capital letters.":PRINT"If you use one l
etter only you will":PRINT"get all entri
es which start with that":PRINT"letter."
:PRINT
960 PRINT"Press ENTER key after typing l
etters."
970 INPUT T$:Y%=LEN(T$):FD%=0
980 WHILE NOT EOF:INPUT#9,Q$
990 INPUT#9,R$,S$,U$:IF LEFT$(Q$,Y%)=T$
THEN PRINT E$(1);": ";Q$+NL$+E$(2);": ";
R$+NL$+E$(3);": ";S$+NL$+E$(4);": ";U$+N
L$:FD%=-1
1000 WEND
1010 IF FD%=0 THEN PRINT"Item not found"
1020 T%=2:GOSUB 1430
```

Figure 6.1. contd.

```
1030 PRINT Z$:" to return.":GOSUB 300
1040 RETURN
1050 REM Sub-menu routines
1060 REM start with add to file.
1070 J%=0:WHILE NOT EOF
1080 GOSUB 1320:J%=J%+1:GOSUB 1330
1090 GOSUB 1340:WEND
1100 J%=J%+1:GOSUB 550:RETURN
1110 CLS:T$="CHANGE ITEM":GOSUB 290
1120 GOSUB 1350:GOSUB 1360:GOSUB 1320:GO
SUB 1330
1130 PRINT Q$+NL$+R$+NL$+S$+NL$+U$
1140 PRINT E$(1);:INPUT Q$:PRINT E$(2);:
INPUT R$
1150 PRINT E$(3);:INPUT S$:PRINT E$(4);:
INPUT U$
1160 WRITE#9,Q$,R$,S$,U$
1170 WHILE NOT EOF
1180 GOSUB 1320:GOSUB 1330
1190 GOSUB 1340:WEND
1200 RETURN
1210 CLS:T$="DELETE ITEM":GOSUB 290
1220 GOSUB 1350:GOSUB 1360
1230 PRINT:PRINT:T$="PLEASE WAIT...":GOS
UB 290
1240 GOSUB 1320:GOSUB 1330
1250 D$=Q$
1260 WHILE NOT EOF:GOSUB 1320:GOSUB 1330
1270 GOSUB 1340:WEND
1280 PRINT:PRINT:T$=D$+" DELETED!":GOSUB
 290:T%=2:GOSUB 1430:RETURN
1290 RETURN
1300 OPENIN F$:OPENOUT F$:RETURN
1310 CLOSEIN:CLOSEOUT:RETURN
1320 INPUT#9,Q$:RETURN
1330 INPUT#9,R$,S$,U$:RETURN
1340 WRITE#9,Q$:WRITE#9,R$,S$,U$:RETURN
1350 PRINT"Please type number of item.";
:INPUT Z%:N%=Z%-1:RETURN
1360 FOR J%=1 TO N%:GOSUB 1320:GOSUB 133
0
1370 GOSUB 1340:NEXT:RETURN
1380 REM Get headings and filename
```

Figure 6.1. contd.

```
1390 OPENIN "HEADS.DAT"
1400 FOR N%=0 TO 4:INPUT #9,E$(N%):NEXT
1410 F$=E$(0):CLOSEIN:RETURN
1420 PRINT"ERROR ";ERR;" IN LINE "; ERL:
GOTO 280
1430 START=TIME:WHILE TIME < START+300*T
%:WEND:RETURN
```

Figure 6.1. contd.

First principles

We shall start by looking at how the program works in outline. Two files are used, both of which are serial files. One short file, called HEADS.DAT, is used to keep a record of your four headings and of the filename for the main file. The purpose of this file is to make the action of the program automatic, so that you don't have to remember a filename or heading names. When you first use the program for a new variety of file, you will format a new disc side, record the program on it, run it so as to type these titles, which stay with the file from then on unless you start another type of file on the same disc side. If you want to use more than one Filing Cabinet, you must keep them on separate discs, or different sides, with a copy of the program on each disc side. The main serial file will carry a filename that you will specify when you first start a file, and it can be of as large a size as will fill a disc. Each record uses either its position number or its first field as a 'key' to finding that record. In other words, you can locate a record by knowing that it is number 58, or by knowing that the first field is surname, and you want to find Carruthers. This scheme is fairly flexible without being too difficult to implement. As I said, this is a skeleton program, and it's yours to trim to shape and pad out as you please. Because of the way that the disc system operates, there is always a backup copy of each file on the disc, with the .BAK extension, which makes the system quite safe to use.

When the program runs, some set-up work is done and you are presented with the main menu. The first time that you use the program on a disc, you should go for the 'Start NEW type of file' option. This allows you to choose four titles for the fields of your records. These names will be recorded and used forever after, so you should plan them carefully. Figure 6.2 shows a typical display. After entering the fields and lengths, you are prompted for a filename. You can choose anything you like, as long as it has eight characters or less, and is not HEADS.DAT. Perhaps you might like to add a line 495 which rejects this name as a filename, and asks again?

Once the filename has been typed and ENTER pressed, the HEADS file is opened and the headings, along with your filename for the main file, will be recorded. At this point, and at several other places in the program, the disc will be busy, and you may have to wait for it. When the file has been created,

```
      New File Specification


Now select your four titles for this
new file, using ENTER after each title.
Only four titles can be used.


First is- ? Name

Name

Second is- ? Address

Address

Third is- ? Age

Age

Fourth is- ? Phone No.

Phone No.

End of titles specification- now we
need a filename of up to eight
characters- no more.



Filename is- friends
```

Figure 6.2. A typical screen display during the entry of titles.

the program returns to the menu. You do *not* have to use this option again unless you decide to keep another different file of data on the same disc. There's nothing wrong with this if your data files are fairly short, but it avoids confusion if you can keep one disc side for each file.

You can now type the first group of data into your file by choosing the 'Start ENTRY in file' option. You don't have to do so at once, of course, because the headings and filename are by now safely on the disc, and you can end the program and switch off if you like. When you go for the entry option, you will be prompted by the field names (such as Address, Name etc.) to type in data. The data will be restricted by line 420 to 38 characters per entry. This has been done to make the screen appearance slightly neater, though data can still spill from one line to the next if both titles and data items are long. Once again, this is something that you can change as you wish. You will find if you enter a lot of data that the disc spins at intervals while you enter data, and you have to wait until the screen cursor is visible again before you can continue typing. To end the entry, you type X, in lower-case or upper-case. If this is inconvenient, change it (line 570)! The whole file will be recorded on the disc, using the filename that you supplied originally. Once again, you can leave the program by selecting option 6 of the menu after you have recorded as many items as you want.

If you select the DELETE, CHANGE or ADD option from the main menu, you will be presented with another menu. This time, the choice is to add to the file, change an item, delete an item, or just return to the main menu. You must not use any of the first three options unless a file has already been created, which is why you have the 'cop-out' option. If you choose to add to the file, the disc drive will read the whole of the file, rerecord it, and then stay open for additions to the file. The items will be correctly numbered, so that you know how many items were on the file, and the number of each item that you add. If you take the CHANGE option, you will be asked to identify which item you want to change, and the identification is by number only in this case (once again, this *could* be changed). When you enter a correct item number, the item is found by reading all of the file up to this point and rewriting it. The item whose number you have requested is then printed on the screen. This allows you to check whether you really want to change the record. There is, however, no drop-out option at this point, and you have to enter items for each field. Perhaps it might be useful to allow pressing ENTER to leave the original item unchanged? If that's what you want, then use an INPUT with a temporary assignment here, test it, and then assign to Q\$, R\$, S\$ or U\$ only if ENTER has not been pressed. When the change has been made, the changed item, and all the rest of the file, is rerecorded. If you choose to delete an item, then once again the item is selected by number, and the file is read and rerecorded as far as the preceding item. The item to be deleted is then read, its title assigned to a variable name, and the rest of the file read and rewritten. The title of the deleted file is then displayed with the information that it has been deleted. Perhaps in this choice you might like to add a piece of routine that lets you read the record and decide whether or not to delete it? If you don't want to delete, then it can be rewritten along with the rest of the file.

Getting back to the main menu, option 4 allows you to list the complete file. When you choose this option, you get another choice, of listing on screen or on the printer. This is done by pressing the S or P keys. For business purposes, this might *always* be a printer option, but if you are using this program for hobby or household interests, you might use only the screen option. Obviously, if you have no printer, you might want to delete the P option. If you take the screen display option, each record is displayed and held for you to inspect. You can press the spacebar to get the next record until the end of the file. You might want to dispense with this, simply using the CPC464's ESC key to prevent the listing running away from you. If the listing is to the printer there are no pauses, the whole listing is printed. Lines 100 to 120 of the program, incidentally, have been kept clear for you to insert any special printer set-up instructions. As we shall see in Chapter 7, the very popular Epson range of printers require some set-up codes if they are to work properly with the CPC464.

Item 5 on the main menu allows you to pick one record for examination. You are then asked if you want to choose by item number or by letters. If you choose by item number, then the program reads the file to the correct place and prints the record whose number you have requested. If you choose to select a name, you are asked to type the name, or the first letter or letters of the name. If you type the whole name, the file will be located only if your typed name agrees *exactly* with the name in the file. You can, however, type just the first letter, and this will result in a list of all the records whose first field starts with this letter. If you type more than one letter, you will get all names which start with these letters – it's rather like using a wildcard in a disc filename. There are no options here for using the printer, nor for looking at one record at a time, but you can add these facilities as you choose.

The program in detail

Now for the hard work. There are many points in this program which are important. If you try to design your own database programs, you will need to know what the disc drive does, and this listing reveals much that isn't exactly made clear by the manual, and which is not so easy to illustrate by short examples. No matter how much you may hate looking at other people's programs it will be useful to study this one, so that you can appreciate reasons for some of the lines. Unless you do so, you can waste a lot of time in your own programming looking at inscrutable error messages and wondering why they arise.

The program is built round a core and a set of subroutines. Much of the programming is straightforward BASIC, and I have made no use of fancy colour or screen presentation effects – there's quite enough to type as it is. Programs for business purposes use the printer for anything important, and the screen is used only for messages to the operator like 'Try putting a disc in the drive'. I'll concentrate on the explanations that relate to the use of the disc drive, rather than explaining everything in detail. In other words, I'm assuming that you knew a reasonable amount of BASIC before you bought a disc drive.

Lines 10 to 130 are concerned with initial values of constants and setting up the system. The first two lines need more explanation than you will find in any of the manuals. Normally, when you open and close buffers, the CPC464 creates space by shifting the top limit of memory. This can create some odd effects in your program, and one of the most puzzling is the corruption of filenames. In this program, the filename for the data is held as a string variable F$. Commands such as OPENIN F$ are then used, but if you follow the normal course that we have outlined so far, you run into trouble with this command. This crops up when you open a file some time after making a menu choice. You may, for example, have defined F$ as 'MYFILE.DAT', but if a choice number 1 on the menu has been made, followed by OPENIN F$, you find that the disc system has been asked to find a file called '1MYFILE.DA', and it can't find it. A second attempt, using CONT, will always succeed, but this can't be done automatically, because disc system errors are not trapped by the usual ON ERROR GOTO statement. Clearing the keyboard buffer does not solve the problem in this case, and the only remedy that I have found is to allocate the buffers permanently, using a set of steps which is mentioned in the *Concise BASIC Specification Manual*. Lines 10 and 20 allow a dummy OPENOUT to shift the memory, and then allocate this limit permanently by using the MEMORY command. The dummy file is then closed again. This method of reserving space permanently for buffers solves all of the curious problems that arise when files are opened and closed.

Line 30 uses an ON ERROR GOTO statement to trap any errors in the BASIC, and ensure that an error will close all files and end the program. This includes syntax errors, so if the program ends when you start to run it, you know you have made a typing error! Line 1420 will analyse the error for you before the shutdown. Always check your data files if you have found an error message, because if this happens in the middle of a change-item action, you will have a data file which is only half full. You will then have to recover the old data file, which will have the .BAK extension. Once the program is up and running, with all mistypings removed, however, you should not find that the error trap ever operates. Lines 70 and 80 contain messages which are used in places, and which you might want to use considerably more. You might also want to use these messages in windows of different colour, to draw more attention to them. Line 90 reads the words which number the headings, and the program starts in earnest in line 140. This prints a title , centred by the GOSUB 290, and asks if you need instructions. The GOSUB 1430 is a time delay routine which will give you a delay of as many seconds as you assign to the integer T%. You are then asked if you need instructions. I have not written *very* detailed instructions, because these just involve another lot of typing. There is enough to remind you of what to do if you have not used the program for some time. You can type your own instructions if you have modified the program for your own use. By allowing the choice of skipping the instructions you can get into the program faster if you use it frequently.

Line 170 clears the screen and then prints the menu. You are asked to select by number, using the GOSUB 300 subroutine and converting to number form with VAL. This number is assigned to K% (an integer) and tested. If the range is acceptable, then lines 210 to 240 carry out the choice. This is not completely straightforward, because choice 1 is very different from the others. It is used *only when a new type of file is to be created*, and it opens the file HEADS.DAT. Because of this, it has to be treated separately. This is done by line 210, and because one choice has been removed from the list in this way, the value of K% has to be reduced by one. If the choice is to be any other item, the program must then check that the data which is contained in file HEADS.DAT is present. This is done in line 220 by testing for the filename F$. If this is a blank, then the file HEADS.DAT must be read, using GOSUB 1390. If you have been using other parts of the program and have returned to the menu, this file will already have been read, and it won't have to be read again. When you reach line 230 you are definitely choosing one of the actions that will need the data file to be opened, so the subroutine which opens the files is used. Line 240 then makes the choice of subroutines, and when the subroutine is finished, line 250 closes the files again. This ensures correct file use unless the program is stopped within a subroutine. Lines 260, 270 give you a chance to return to the menu unless you have picked the 'END program' option. The subroutines carry out all of the main actions. This is important, because it makes the program very easy to change. Practically all the subroutines that you might need for your own 'custom' version are listed, so if you know in detail what each subroutine does, making your own version is relatively easy.

The creation subroutine

The subroutine that starts in line 440 creates a completely new file. This will wipe out any other file that has been created with this program on the same disc side, which is why it is useful to have several copies of the program on different disc sides. The loop that starts in line 460 gets title names for each field. The INPUT stage for this is handled by a separate subroutine in line 420, which allows the length of title to be tested. You might want to use this subroutine also to test changes to the file. Each title and length is assigned to an array variable E$, with four items. As always, you can change this to suit yourself. If all is well, then you are asked for a filename in lines 480, 490. Once again, it might be useful to test this to make sure that the name HEADS was not used, and that no extension is placed on this name. Line 510 adds the extension of DAT, and assigns this also to E$(0). This allows the headings and the filename to be recorded by one loop in line 520. When this has been done, the program returns in line 530 – in this case, the return will be to the GOTO 260 command in line 210. You can then either return to the menu, or end the program. Your titles and filename are now recorded, and the program is now ready to make use of this new file. You will *not* make use of this menu option again until you come to choose another subject for filing.

Writing to the file

Selecting the 'START entry in file' option in the main menu leads to the subroutine which starts in line 540. If this option is selected, this will replace any existing file. It is used, therefore, just after a new file has been created by the use of option 1. If you want to add items to a file, then option 3 should be used. Line 550 gives brief instructions, and the titles of each field are printed from the array E$ as reminders. No attempt has been made to restrict the size of each entry, and you might want to do this for yourself. For a new file, the record number J% has been assigned with starting number 1 in line 80. The test at the end of line 570 checks for the entry of the letter X as the first field, because this terminates the entry. Line 630 will then correct the count number, and the subroutine returns. When it returns, the action of closing files will ensure that all data has been recorded. The write line is in 610, and this uses WRITE#9 rather than PRINT#9. The reason is that WRITE#9 allows strings to be separated more easily when the output is in a form such as WRITE#9,R$,S$,U$. If PRINT#9 is used in such a case, then the read (using INPUT#9,R$,S$,U$) will *not* separate the items correctly. Our examples so far have used PRINT#9 in a loop, which has side-stepped this problem. Note that when X is used to terminate an entry, this letter is *not* recorded.

Once a file has been opened with menu choice 1, and written to with menu choice 2, it can be further used by choices 3, 4 and 5. You would not normally use choices 1 and 2 again, but the remaining choices will come in for heavy use from now on. We'll start with the 'heavyweight' item, choice 3. This allows addition to a file, alteration of a record, or deletion of a record. So that all of these actions can be catered for, this menu choice leads to another menu in line 650. This in turn leads to three more subroutines.

Choosing addition to a file leads to the subroutine in line 1070. Since the files are serial, adding to a file really means reading and rewriting the whole of the existing file, and then leaving the file open so that more items can be added. The reading and rewriting of the existing file is done by the WHILE...WEND loop in lines 1070 to 1090. In this loop, the counter variable J% is used to count the records as they are read and rewritten. Line 1100 then increments J%, and calls the original entry subroutine so that more items can be added. As before, entering the letter X as the first field of a record will terminate the addition of records. The rest of the file is written, and the files are closed when the routine returns.

When you take the 'change' option of this extra menu, you have to specify which item is to be changed. The subroutine starts in line 1110 with its title, and then calls the subroutine at line 1350 to find the number of the item. This is a convenient method from the point of view of easy programming, but if you want to find the item by letter, then a method will be studied later. When the number is specified, Z% is set to a value of one less than this chosen number. The subroutine at line 1360 is then used to read and rewrite all records up to this item. The chosen record is then read, using the GOSUBs at the end of line 1120. Line 1130 then displays the record, and lines 1140 and 1150 are used to change each field of the record. You could use a more elaborate routine here, allowing the ENTER key with no entry to mean that the field should be unchanged. You might also want to add the option of leaving the whole record unchanged if you decide that you don't want to change it after all. Line 1160 writes the changed record to the buffer, and lines 1170 to 1190 write the rest of the file.

Listing the file

The file listing option in the main menu leads to line 690, prints the title of the choice, and asks for the options of screen or printer. This choice is made by pressing the S or P keys, and the choice is tested in line 720. The result causes Z% to be assigned with 0 for screen listing, or 8 for printer listing. This allows the expression PRINT#Z% to be used to give either type of output. The items are printed one on each line, with the item number. This item number can be used also in picking individual items for changing or deleting, using option 3. In line 770, if Z%=0, meaning screen output, the listing stops after each item to give you time to read it. You could, if you like, modify this so that you have the choice of paused or continuous listing. Listing to the printer is *always* continuous.

When the fifth option, to pick an item, is chosen, the subroutine which starts at line 790 is used. This prompts for a choice of number or letter selection, which is made in lines 830, 840. These are dealt with by separate subroutines, with the number choice routine starting in line 860. Taking this option first, the number is entered, and the two subroutines at 1320 and 1330 are used to input the fields, using a WHILE...WEND loop rather than a FOR...NEXT because of the ease of detecting an impossible record number. If the item is found, then line 890 will print it and break the loop. If it is not found, then the EOF marker operates the WEND and the message in line 910 is printed.

If the letter selection method is chosen, the subroutine starts at line 950 with brief instructions. The letter or group of letters is entered in line 970, and the number of characters is assigned to Y%. The 'marker' variable FD% is also set to zero. A loop starts in line 980 which will input each field name and compare a number of letters equal to Y% with the letters that you have entered. If these two are identical, then all of the fields of the record are printed and FD% is changed to −1. The loop continues over the whole file, because there may be more than one entry which uses the same letter or group of letters. Line 1010 will print the message only if no item has been found, using the value of FD% to indicate this.

The last menu option is simply to end the program. This is necessary, because it provides a way of ending without having to carry out any of the other menu actions which would open files. You should *never* have to end a program by pressing the ESC key twice, because this can result in the program leaving files open, and so leaving you with an incomplete data file on the disc. This has been avoided in this case by having ON BREAK GOSUB 280 in line 30. This ensures that pressing ESC twice will cause the program to end by carrying out line 280, rather than by breaking, and it therefore safeguards the files *to some extent*. The safeguard is not perfect, however, because it depends where you break. If you are deleting an item, for example, part of the file will have been read and passed to the output buffer. If you break at this point, the first part of the file will be saved, but the second part will not. You will then have to use the .BAK copy to restore your file. To do so, delete the new copy, and rename the .BAK file with the name of the file which should be the new file. You still have the .BAK copy as your backup.

That's all there is to it. Taken as a whole, it looks rather intimidating, but when you split it into core and subroutines, as it was when it was written, it looks a lot simpler. It's by no means a polished piece of programming. You'll find, for example, that more use could be made of subroutines in some sections. You'll certainly find that you will want to modify parts of the program to suit your own needs. It's yours now, so modify it as you wish, but please don't sell it or publish it as your own work!

Chapter Seven
Printers

Whenever your use of a computer extends beyond playing games that other people have written, there are two additions to your computer equipment that you will urgently want. One of these is a disc system, and that's a topic that has filled the first six chapters of this book. The next must be a printer. In many cases, particularly when you are developing your own programs, the printer has an even higher priority than the use of the disc system.

The reasons for using a printer are obvious if you use the machine for business purposes. You can hardly expect your accountants or your income tax inspector to look at accounts that can be shown only on the screen. It would be a total waste of time if you kept your stock records with a computer, and then had to write down each change on a piece of paper, copying from the display on the screen. For all of these purposes, and particularly for word processing, the printer is an essential part of the computer system. Output on paper is referred to as 'hard copy', and this hard copy is essential if the computer is be of any use in business applications. For word processing uses, it's not enough just to have a printer; you need a printer with a high-quality output with characters as clear as those of a first-class electric typewriter.

Even if your computer is never used for any kind of business purpose, however, you can run up against the need for a printer. If you use, modify or write programs, the printer can pay for itself in terms of your time. Trying to trace what a program does from a listing which you can view only a few lines at a time on the screen is totally frustrating. Quite apart from anything else, if your use of BASIC on the CPC464 relies a lot on the use of GOTO for loops, you might have to list a dozen different pieces of a program just to find where one GOTO might lead you. The answer is to avoid the use of GOTO, but there are times when FOR...NEXT and WHILE...WEND loops are not completely satisfactory substitutes. The problem is even worse if you write your own programs. Even a very modest program may need a hundred lines of BASIC, some of which may be long lines. Trying to check a program of a hundred lines when you may be able to see only a dozen or so at a time on the screen is like bailing out a leaky boat with a teaspoon. With a printer attached to your CPC464 you can print out the whole listing, and then examine it at your leisure. If you design your programs the way you ought to, using a 'core' and subroutines, then you can print each subroutine on a separate piece of paper. In this way, you can keep a note of each different subroutine, with variable names noted. On each sheet you can write what the subroutine does, what quantities are represented by the variable names, and how it is used. If you have a utility program that allows you to merge subroutines, you can then construct programs painlessly using your library of tested subroutines.

Printer types

Granted, then, that the use of a printer is a high priority for the really serious computer user, what sort of printers are available? The CPC464 uses the almost universal Centronics connection for printers, including the Amstrad printers which appear to be made by Seikosha. It's difficult to imagine any 'serious' computer without a Centronics interface, for this is the connection method that is used by all the famous-name printers which are available. This means that you can attach almost any good-quality printer that you like to the CPC464. This opens up the way for the use of any of the printers which are offered at such attractive prices in the magazines. In particular, it allows you to use printers such as the Epson and Juki range.

Printers that are used with small computers will use one of the mechanisms listed in Figure 7.1. Of these, the impact dot matrix type is the most common. A dot matrix printer creates each character out of a set of dots, and when you look at the print closely, you can see the dot structure.

Dot matrix
   impact
   thermal
electrostatic

Type impact
   type stalk
   daisywheel

Plotters
   graphics printers
   X-Y plotters

Ink-jet
   single colour
   multicolour

Figure 7.1. A list of printer mechanism types.

The printhead of the dot matrix printer consists of a set of tiny electromagnets, each of which acts on a set of needles that are arranged in a vertical line (Figure 7.2). By firing these needles at an inked ribbon which is placed between the head and the paper, dots can be marked on the paper.

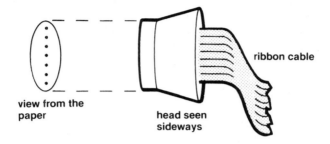

Figure 7.2. Illustrating a dot matrix printhead.

Each character is printed by firing some needles, moving the head slightly, then firing another set of needles, and so on until the character shape is drawn completely (Figure 7.3). The most common pattern of dots for low-cost printers is the 7×5, meaning that the characters can be made out of up to seven dots in height and up to five in width. This implies that the head

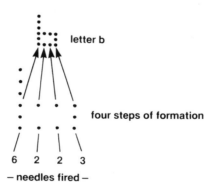

Figure 7.3. How a 7×5 dot matrix head creates a character.

moves across the paper in five steps to print each character, and that up to seven needles can be fired. Using a 7×5 structure gives characters which are readable, but not good-looking. The dots are very evident, and some of the letters are misshapen. You will find, for example, that lower-case letters lack 'descenders'. This means the tails on letters y,g,p,q will either be missing, or will be on the same level as the foot of other letters. When this print is used for listings which are in upper-case only, there is no problem. You would not, however, use a printer of this class to print letters or other documents that anyone else would have to read.

Rather better results can be obtained if the number of needles in the printhead is increased. Using 9×9 (nine needles, nine steps across) or 15×9 heads can create much better-looking characters, lower-case or upper-case. Another advantage of these printheads is that the characters are not limited to the ordinary letters of the alphabet and the numbers. Foreign characters can usually be printed, and it is possible to print Arabic script, or to make up your own character set, for example. Most of the dot matrix printers are impact types. This means what is says, that the paper is marked by the impact of a needle on an inked ribbon which hits the paper. There are also thermal and electrostatic dot matrix printers. These use needles, but the needles do not move. Instead the needles are used to affect a special type of paper. In the electrostatic printer (such as the old ZX printer), the needles are used to pass sparks to the paper, removing a thin coating of metal from the black backing paper. The thermal type of printer uses hot needles to make marks on heat-sensitive paper. Both of these printers require expensive special paper, and are unsuitable for serious business purposes, so we won't spend any time on them here. If you want a cheap printer for listings, there are better methods.

The ultimate in print quality at the moment is provided by the daisywheel printer. This uses a typewriter approach, with the letters and other characters placed on stalks round a wheel. The principle is that the wheel spins to bring the letter that you want to the top, and then a small hammer hits the back of the letter, pressing it against the ribbon and on to the paper. Because this is exactly the same way that a typewriter produces text, the quality of print is very high. It's also possible now to buy a combination of typewriter and daisywheel printer. This looks like a typewriter, with a normal typewriter keyboard, but has an interface connection for a computer. You can use it as a typewriter, and then connect it to the computer and use it as a printer. Machines of this sort are made by leading typewriter manufacturers such as Silver Reed, Brother, Triumph Adler, Smith Corona, and others. If you need a typewriter as well as a printer, then this type of machine is an obvious choice.

The third kind of mechanism that we shall look at here is the graphics printer. This is a remarkable mechanism which uses four miniature ball pens to mark the paper direct, with no ribbon. It can be used for graphics work, and when it is used as a printer, the letters are *drawn* rather than printed. Because four pens are used, the markings can be in four different colours. Printers of this type are not expensive (as printers go) and can be very useful, particularly if you want graphics output in colour. Another type of printer that is now becoming available is the ink-jet printer, which operates by shooting fine jets of ink at the paper. This one shares the disadvantage of the thermal and the electrostatic types in that you obtain only one copy. Impact printers have the great advantage that you can obtain an extra copy by using a sheet of carbon paper and another sheet of plain paper. You can also buy listing paper which has a built-in carbon, or which uses the NCR (no carbon required) principle to produce two copies.

Interfaces

The printer has to be connected by a cable to the computer, so that signals can be passed in each direction. The computer will pass to the printer the signals that make the printer produce characters on the paper, but the printer must also be able to pass signals to the computer. This is because the printer operates much more slowly than the computer. Unless the printer contains a large memory 'buffer', so that it can store all the signals from the computer and then get to work on them at its own pace, some sort of 'handshaking' is needed. This means that the printer will accept as many signals as its memory will take, and then will send out a signal to the computer which makes the computer hang up. When the printer has completed a number of characters, (one line, one thousand, or possibly just one character), it changes the 'handshake' signal, and the computer sends another batch. This continues until all of the text has been printed. This can mean that you don't have the use of the computer until the printer has finished. Printers can be very slow, particularly daisywheel and plotter types. Even the fastest dot matrix printers can make you wait for a minute or more for a listing.

Two types of interface are used by practically all printers. These are classed as serial or parallel. A parallel printer is connected to the computer by a cable which uses a large number of separate strands. Since each character in ASCII code uses seven signals, the parallel printer sends these along seven separate strands – many printers can use an eighth signal and this is usually sent as well. In addition, there are cable strands for the 'handshake' signals. The best-known, and most used variety of parallel connection is called Centronics, after the printer manufacturer which first used it. Practically all of the popular printers use this type of parallel interface.

The serial interface sends the signals out one at a time. This means that at least seven signals have to be sent for each character, and in practice the total must be ten or eleven, to allow for start and stop signals which are used to mark where the signals for each character start and stop. This system uses less cabling, because only two strands need to be used for signals, and the cables can be longer because there's no risk of one signal interfering with another. The standard system is called RS-232. Printers can be obtained with RS-232, but seldom as standard, and often only as an extra, costing up to an additional £50.

The Amstrad CPC464 uses a parallel system, so that practically all of the popular printers can be connected in addition to the Amstrad printer. The

Amstrad DMP-1 printer is a simple design which produces acceptable results for listings. Its work can be seen in the examples that appear in the Disc Manual. For business use, however, it's unlikely that this standard of print would be acceptable. The Amstrad printer, however, can reproduce the CPC464 graphics shapes, and this might be important to you. If, however, I make the assumption that you wouldn't buy the disc drive unless you were interested in business applications of some sort, then it makes sense if I confine the descriptions here to printers with high-quality output.

In this book, for example, the listings have been reproduced on an Epson RX80 printer. This uses a 9×9 matrix for characters, so that the appearance of the characters is better. In addition, the Epson can operate in 'emphasised' mode. In this printing mode, each dot is struck twice, but the head is shifted slightly between dots. This causes the dots to look almost joined up, and makes the appearance of the print much more acceptable.

A problem that you are bound to run up against when you use any non-Amstrad printer is that of line feed and carriage return. Many computers send out only one code number, the carriage return code (13) at the end of a line. Other machines send both the line feed (code 10) and carriage return codes. Printers are arranged, therefore, so that either possibility can be catered for by a switch. If you connect your printer and find that everything is printed on one line, then don't return the printer. Just look in the Manual, and find the switch that alters the line feed setting. If on the other hand you find that each line is double-spaced, then this switch will have to be set to the opposite position. My CPC464, when connected to an Epson MX80, performed two line feeds no matter how the selector switch was set, and this had to be corrected by a rather roundabout method, noted later in this chapter.

The Epson MX80, FX80 and RX80

The Epson range of printers has for a long time been the most popular range of moderately-priced printers, offering excellent print quality at reasonable prices. The RX80 and FX80 are the latest in this line, but if you are offered a second-hand MX80, then this also is a good buy. A particular feature of the Epson range is that the printheads plug into place, and can easily be replaced when they wear out. My old Epson MX80 was just beginning to show signs of head wear after printing half-a-million words, so it might not be a problem for you!

The standard version of the RX80 uses pin-feed, but the RX80F/T can take any form or paper, including rolls. You have to pay extra for a paper roll holder, but if you are handy with wood and piano wire, this is something that you could easily make for yourself. The advantage of using the F/T version is that plain unperforated paper rolls are *very* much cheaper to buy, and it also means that you can use plain paper sheets if you want to. When you use a lot of paper for listings, this can be a great saving. Paper width of 4″ to 10″ in pin feed or plain form can be used, so you can buy whatever paper size is on offer. If you use the F/T option, you can then buy the teletype rolls, which are 8½ inches wide.

The RX80 offers a full set of upper or lower-case letters, and you don't have to go through any elaborate antics to select which one you want. Figure 7.4 shows the normal upper-case letters of the RX80, as you would use them

```
10 REM USING RX80 IN NORMAL MODE
20 REM WHICH PRINTS AT MAXIMUM SPEED
```

Figure 7.4. The normal characters of the Epson RX80.

for a listing. The print speed is very fast, and most listings will be completed in under a minute. Figure 7.5 shows the lower-case letters, which are much better formed than those of cheaper printers. Figure 7.6 shows the 'emphasised' print of the RX80. This is achieved by typing PRINT#8,CHR$(27)CHR$(69) (press ENTER) before listing. The emphasised print can be cancelled by using PRINT#8,CHR$(27)CHR$(70).

```
10 rem lower case on the screen
20 rem can also be produced on the printer.
```

Figure 7.5. The lower-case characters of the Epson RX80.

```
10 REM THIS SHOWS THE EMPHASISED
20 REM STYLE OF PRINT OF THE RX80
```

Figure 7.6. The emphasised print of the RX80.

These commands can be used in programs, so that you can print normal, condensed, emphasised, double width, and all of the other varieties, under program control. This makes it very easy to produce good headings, produce words in bold type or italics, and to underline. For a lot of word processing actions, the RX80 can be a very satisfactory low-cost alternative to a daisywheel. International character sets (for the USA, France, Germany, England, Denmark, Sweden, Italy, Spain, Japan, Norway) can be printed, and are under software control. This means that selection is made by printing CHR$ numbers rather than by altering switches on the printer itself. The only switches that you have to alter are for such items as are listed in Figure 7.7. For many purposes, you would probably never need to alter the factory settings of these switches. Figure 7.8 shows the options that can be selected by sending CHR$(27)CHR$(N) codes to the printer.

Switch 1

Position	ON	OFF
1	Condensed	Pica (print size)
2	Graphics	Control code
3	No buzzer	Buzzer on (end of paper)
4	12 inch	11 inch (form length)
5	Not detected	Detected (paper end)
6 ⎫	Selects from international	
7 ⎬	character set of	
8 ⎭	eight languages	

Switch 2

Position	ON	OFF
1	Slashed	Non-slashed (zero)
2	Control pin	Not fixed
3	Line feed	No line feed (with C/R)
4	Skip	Don't skip (perforation)

Figure 7.7. List of RX80 switch settings.

Each of the letter codes will be preceded by CHR$(27), the ESC code. Some of the CHR$(number) codes can be used alone – consult the manual for details.

Code	Effect
J	Adjust line spacing in 1/216 inch units.
M	Elite size characters.
P	Pica size characters.
CHR$(14)	Enlarged print.
CHR$(20)	Cancel enlarged print.
W	Second enlarged print mode.
CHR$(15)	Condensed print.
CHR$(18)	Cancel condensed print.
_	Underline on/off switch.
E	Set emphasised mode.
F	Cancel emphasised mode.
G	Double strike mode.
H	Cancel double strike mode.
S	Superscript/subscript switch.
T	Cancel superscript/subscript.
CHR$(8)	Backspace.
CHR$(4)	Alternate character set.

CHR$(5)	Cancel alternate character set.
m	Choose graphics or control characters.
0	1/8 inch line spacing.
1	7/72 inch line spacing.
2	1/6 inch line spacing.
3	Set spacing in 1/216 inch units.
A	Set line spacing in 1/72 inch units.
CHR$(9)	Horizontal tab.
CHR$(11)	Vertical tab.
e	Tab unit setting.
f	Skip position setting.
C	Form length setting.
N	Skip over perforation setting.
O	Skip over perforation cancel.
Q	Right margin set.
I	Left margin set.
8	Ignore paper end detector.
9	Enable paper end detector.
<	One line unidirectional printing.
@	Restore normal settings.
U	Unidirectional printing.
S	Half speed (quiet!) printing.

Other codes can be used to control each pin in the head so that graphics can be printed. This allows 'screen dump' programs which place a copy of the screen graphics on to the paper to be written for this printer.

Figure 7.8. The software selections of the RX80.

The line-feed fix

When the CPC464 is used along with any of the Epson printers which I have tried, it causes double line feeds no matter what the setting of the line feed switch in the printer happens to be. This is not a problem with the Amstrad printer, nor is it a worry with the Juki or Tandy printers (described later in this chapter). Fortunately, it can be fixed with a bit of software magic. The Epson printers allow the distance between lines to be changed in units of 1/72 inch. This is done by sending the codes ESC "A", followed by the number of 1/72 inch steps. For the CPC464, a line feed of 7/72 inch is sufficient to make the double line feed into an acceptable size, so the command:

PRINT#8,CHR$(27);"A";CHR$(7)

will carry this out. It can, however, lead to odd effects when a line of a listing spills over onto another line. To avoid this, you have to ensure that the computer sends out line feeds at the correct number of characters. Suppose, for example, that your printer will line feed each 80th character. You must ensure that the CPC464 does the same by the command: WIDTH 80. If this is not done, the printer will perform its own single small line feed, making the lines too close to each other. The listings in this book were produced with WIDTH 40, and with the printer forced to work with 40-column lines by using:

?#8,CHR$(27)"Q";CHR$(40)

These codes are used by both the MX80 and the RX80 printers. This is important, because not all of the printer control codes are identical for the different Epson models. It's a good idea to keep some printer setting programs on a disc, so that you can RUN one as you choose to suit whatever printer you happen to be using.

The Juki 6100 daisywheel

The Juki was one of the first low-cost daisywheel printers to become available. Like most printers, it comes with a Centronics parallel interface, though an RS-232 serial interface is available at extra cost. The Juki is a large and very heavy machine which can accept paper up to 13" wide. The daisywheel is of the same type as is used on Triumph Adler printers, and the ribbon cartridge is an IBM Selectric 82/C type. The ribbon that was supplied with my Juki was of the 'single-strike' variety, and this had a very short life (about three chapters of this book!). A 'multistrike' type of ribbon is much better. With the latter, the whole width of the ribbon is used by moving the cartridge up and down as well as by moving the ribbon itself. These ribbons are very easy to obtain from many suppliers, but the best prices I have seen have been in the Inmac catalogue. The ribbons are carbon film rather than inked nylon, and are thrown away after use. This always seem a pity, because the cartridge contains mechanisms that look as if it could easily be used again. Some day, I'll try reloading one of these cartridges.

The printhead of the Juki will print in either direction, and there is a 2K buffer. This means that short pieces of text can be transferred to the printer buffer almost instantly, and the computer can be used for other purposes while the printer gets on with the printing actions. Printing is much slower than the normal rate of the Epson, but not so much slower than the emphasised mode of the Epson as to make the daisywheel seem irritatingly slow. Its enormous advantage is the quality of the type. This is exceptionally clear on the top copy, and even three carbons later it is still very legible. For any letter work, or for the manuscript of a book, the Juki is ideal.

As you would expect of any modern design of printer, the Juki permits many character sets, but you need to have the appropriate daisywheels fitted for each language. You cannot, for example, have words in alternate character sets without changing wheels in between. Changing wheels is particularly simple, but this is something that you don't have to worry about with dot matrix printers, because the same dot matrix head can produce any character under software control. The Juki allows underlining, bold type, and shadow type in addition to the normal printing style, and you can select your print style from a range of at least fourteen daisywheels. The daisy wheels are expensive in comparison with others on the market, but ribbons are cheap. Figure 7.9 shows a printout from the Juki with the standard Courier daisywheel fitted. By removing the top cover, you can gain access to a set of miniature switches. Switch No. 1 controls auto line feed, and for use with the CPC464 this must be set to the OFF position. This will give correct line-spacing – the ON position causes each line to be double-spaced. The switch-change must be done with the machine switched off. This is not so much because of risk but because these switch settings have *no effect* until the machine is switched off and then on again.

```
10 REM DEMONSTRATION OF JUKI
20 PRINT#8,"This is JUKI normal print"
30 PRINT#8,CHR$(27);"E";"This is underli
ned";CHR$(27);"R"
40 PRINT#8,"We can change";CHR$(27);"O";
" to bold print."
50 PRINT#8,"We can change ";CHR$(27);"W"
;"to shadow print."
60 REM The C/R clears these effects
70 PRINT#8,CHR$(27);"Y";CHR$(27);"Z";CHR
$(27)"H";CHR$(27);"I";CHR$(27);"J";CHR$(
27);"K"
```

```
This is JUKI normal print
This is underlined
We can change to bold print.
We can change to shadow print.
```

Figure 7.9. The printing of the Juki daisywheel, using the Courier 10 daisywheel.

Like the Epson, the Juki permits a number of changes to be made simply by sending control codes to the printer. These use the ESC character, CHR$(27) followed by one more character, so that whatever immediately follows CHR$(27) is never printed. The options include graphics mode, left and right margins, lines per page, half-line feeds in either direction (for printing subscripts and superscripts), top and bottom page margins, and some special characters, including the English pound sign. Even more

Each of these codes will be preceded by CHR$(27).

Code	Effect
1	Set horizontal tab (HT) at present position.
2	Clear all tabs.
3	Graphics mode on (C/R clears).
4	Graphics mode off.
5	Forward print on (C/R clears).
6	Backward print on (C/R clears).
7	Print suppress on (C/R clears).
8	Clear present HT stop.
9	Set left margin at present position.
0	Set right margin at present position.
CHR$(9)	Set HT (tab number follows).
CHR$(10)	Set lines per page (number follows).
CHR$(11)	Vertical tab (VT) set (number follows).
CHR$(12)	Set lines per page (number follows).
_	Sets VT at present position.
CHR$(13)P	Remote reset.
CHR$(30)	Sets line spacing (number follows).
CHR$(31)	Sets character spacing.
C	Clears top/bottom margins.
D	Reverse half-line feed.
U	Normal half-line feed.
L	Sets bottom margin at present position.
T	Sets top margin at present position.
Y	Special character.
Z	Special character.
H	Special character (new paragraph symbol).
I	English pound sign.
J	Diaeresis mark.
K	Spanish c with cedilla.
/	Automatic backward print.
\	Disable backward print.
S	Set character spacing.
CHR$(26)A	Remote error reset.
CHR$(26)I	Initialise printer.
CHR$(26)1	Status (serial interface only).
P	Proportional spacing on.
Q	Proportional spacing off.
CHR$(17)	Offset selection.
E	Underline on.
R	Underline off.
O	Bold print on (C/R clears).
W	Shadow print on (C/R clears).

&	Bold or shadow print off.
%	Carriage settling time.
N	Clear carriage settling time.
CHR$(8)	1/120 inch back space.
X	Cancels all word processing modes except proportional spacing.

Figure 7.10. The software selections of the Juki.

usefully, the print can be changed to bold or shadow by sending such codes, and text can be underlined. Figure 7.10 lists these actions.

The same quality of print can now be obtained from a large number of daisywheel typewriters, and many of these now have a Centronics parallel interface. This type of machine offers a lot of advantages, because it can be used as a typewriter for small items that do not justify the use of the computer, yet it is available for word processing use along with the CPC464 and such programs as AMSWORD. These machines can now be bought in the high street stores as well as from office supply shops. The only thing to watch is that replacement ribbons and daisywheels are obtainable from several different sources. There's nothing worse than being stuck with a machine for which you can obtain spares from only one supplier.

The CGP-115 4-colour graphics printer

One of the most popular small graphics printer mechanisms is made under the trademark of ALPS. It's Japanese, and in place of the mechanisms that are used by most printers, it actually *draws* its characters with a set of four miniature ball pens. The reason for the set of four is that this allows printing in four different colours – black, blue, red and green. The mechanism is made into boxed units by many manufacturers, and sold under a wide variety of names, but it is most easily obtained from Tandy stores under the Tandy code number of CGP-115. This version includes both a Centronics and a serial interface, which makes the printer usable on practically any microcomputer which uses reasonably standard interfaces. Since the Tandy stores offer a good service on spares (pens, paper, etc.) and trouble-shooting, it makes sense to buy the Tandy version as there is a Tandy store in most large towns. In addition to being used as a printer, however, this machine acts as a graphics plotter, and you can draw diagrams and other pictures by means of instructions sent from *any* computer. This applies even if the computer has no graphics capabilities of its own.

The CGP-115 in detail

The printer uses a plain paper roll which is 4.5 inches wide. Tandy stores sell 3 rolls, each about 145 to 150 feet long, for just under £5. These paper rolls are also used by a wide variety of adding machines, so if you haunt your local office supply stores, you may find alternative sources at lower prices. The paper is tightly gripped by the printer, because it is moved around a lot in the course of printing. The printing carriage consists of a holder which is loaded with four miniature ball pens. This holder can be rotated so that one pen is touching the paper. Printing is achieved by moving the pen holder from side to side, and the paper up and down, and is such a fascinating sight that you'll probably print listings over and over again just for the pleasure of watching the mechanism! I know that I did. When the printer is switched on, it goes into a 'pen-test' routine, slowly drawing a square in each colour so that you can check that none of the pens has run dry. They have a surprisingly long life, and each pack of 3 pens costs around £1.99 from Tandy stores. You won't find alternative supplies quite so easily in this case!

Normally, the CGP-115 acts as a printer, and you can use it to print listings. It is not by any stretch of the imagination a fast printer, even compared with a daisywheel but the results are much easier to read than some dot matrix output. The enormous advantage of using the Tandy printer, however, is that it can be used as a graphics plotter. This means that if you send suitable instructions to the printer, it will draw diagrams. The instructions are not the same as the graphics instructions of the CPC464 (or any other computer), but this is not a disadvantage. If at some stage you change to another computer, the Tandy printer will still be useful, and the graphics programs that you have used with the CPC464 can easily be adapted to another computer. This is very useful to know if your household is on the verge of becoming a two-computer family. The CGP-115 has a small set of four switches at the back which can be used for setting up the printer. For the CPC464, the settings of the switches are: 1.OFF 2.ON 3.OFF 4.ON. This gives the correct line feed and the normal size of print with the parallel interface in use.

The Tandy CGP-115 commands

Because this book is mainly concerned with the use of the Amstrad disc drive and several different printers, I have had to resist the temptation to add several chapters on the Tandy graphics printer. Many CPC464 owners, however, will probably want to make use of this type of printer mechanism, which is sold under a variety of other brand names. For business applications, for example, the ability of the CGP-115 to produce graphs in four colours is extremely useful for such a modestly-priced unit. The following is a list of the commands which are available when the Tandy version is used. The commands are shown in their CPC464 form. Figure 7.11 demonstrates the use of these commands in printing a name in four different directions.

```
10 REM DIRECTIONS
20 PRINT#8,CHR$(18)
30 PRINT#8,"M50,0"
40 INPUT"Your name, please ";NM$
50 PRINT#8,"P";NM$
60 PRINT#8,"Q1"
70 PRINT#8,"P";NM$
80 PRINT#8,"Q2"
90 PRINT#8,"P";NM$
100 PRINT#8,"Q3"
110 PRINT#8,"P";NM$
120 PRINT#8,"Q0"
130 PRINT#8,"A"
140 END
```

Figure 7.11. A printout from the Tandy CGP-115 graphics printer.

PRINT#8,CHR$(8)	Move one space left (backspace). Used in text mode.
PRINT#8,CHR$(11)	Reverse line feed – move paper down by one line in text mode.
PRINT#8,CHR$(17)	Select text mode from graphics mode.
PRINT#8,CHR$(18)	Select graphics mode from text mode.
PRINT#8,CHR$(29)	Change colour in text mode.

Graphics commands

The following letters can be sent when the printer is in *graphics* mode. The letters are *not* printed; instead, they are used as commands. Several of these commands must be followed by numbers, such as X, Y coordinate numbers, to specify positions. All of these letters would be sent to the printer by using PRINT#8, after executing PRINT#8,CHR$(18).

A	Reset pen to left margin, no line drawn, return to text mode.
Cn	Change colour of pen. n is colour number, 0 to 8.
Dx,y	Draw from present position to point x,y. Can be extended to more than one point.
H	Move pen to origin without drawing a line. The origin is a specified starting point.
I	Set new origin at current pen position. If you want a new origin at point 5,10, then place the pen there, and PRINT#8, "I"
Jx,y	Jump, or draw-relative. Draws a line from present position to one x steps to the right and y steps up. Do not confuse this with D, which draws to the *absolute* point x,y.
Ln	Change line type. If n=0, the line is solid, but using numbers 1 to 15 will draw various dotted lines.
Mx,y	Move to point x,y without drawing a line.
Pchars	Print the following characters while the printer is in graphics mode. The size of the characters can be controlled, and characters can be printed vertically or backwards.
Qdir	Change print direction. The number dir, can be in the range 0 to #8. 0 gives normal printing, 1 gives top to bottom, 2 gives upside down, 8 gives bottom to top
Rx,y	Relative move. Move pen, without drawing, to a point x steps to the right and y steps up. Using −x moves left, using −y moves down.
Sn	Selects size of characters to be printed. n must be between 0 and #8.
Xa,b,c	Draw graph axis. n is 0 for a Y axis, 1 for X axis. The distance between marks on the axis is specified by b, which must be between −999 and +999. The number of steps is c, between 1 and 255.

Chapter Eight
Disc Utility Programs

A disc utility program is one that is intended to make your use of discs easier, especially if you want to do rather more than just load and save. In particular, disc utilities allow you to see what is stored on the discs, including information which is not normally available to you and which cannot be obtained by normal load operations. The most important disc utility is one which allows you to look at any sector of any track. This allows you to see what is stored on the CP/M reserved tracks, for example, and to find where programs are stored. It can also be used to read a disc which, because of partial demagnetisation, for example, will no longer load correctly. If a disc editor program is also available, the correct bytes can *sometimes* be replaced so as to make the disc usable again. I must stress, though, that this is a desperate measure. You would normally have a backup of any disc, and if a disc became unusable, you would normally reformat it, back up the other copy on to it, and then continue. Human nature being what it is, however, a disc editor is still useful at times, and an editing program has been included in this chapter. Another function is that of deliberately making a disc difficult to copy, and for such protection you need to be able to carry out disc editing. This chapter, then, is concerned with various disc utilities. Most of these make use of machine code to achieve disc reading or writing, but the programs themselves are in BASIC, with the machine code poked into memory. You need no knowledge of machine code either to enter the programs or to use them. Obviously, if you are going to go further into the workings of the disc operating system, you will have to use machine code. For readers who have already seen my book *Introducing Amstrad CPC464 Machine Code*, I have added a listing and a short explanation of the machine code part of each program.

Read track and sector

This utility program, listed in Figure 8.1, will allow you to read any sector of a CPC464 CP/M disc. You should type in the program as usual – the listing has been produced with a printer setting of forty characters per line so that

```
10 CLS:GOSUB 500:GOSUB 600
20 PRINT#1,TAB(13)"Track & Sector.":PRIN
T#1,TAB(13);STRING$(14,"_")
30 PRINT#0:PRINT#0,"TRACK No.- (0 to 39)
":INPUT T%
40 IF T%<0 OR T%>39 THEN K%=39:GOSUB 800
:GOTO 30
50 PRINT#0:PRINT#0,"SECTOR No. (0 to 8)
":INPUT S%
60 IF S%<0 OR S%>8 THEN K%=8:GOSUB 800:G
OTO 50
70 S%=S%+1+&40:D%=T%*256+S%
80 CALL &A000,D%
90 CLS#0:CLS#1
100 PRINT#1:PRINT#1,TAB(8)"Byte No.";TAB
(20)"Hex";TAB(27)"Char"
110 PRINT#2:PRINT#2,TAB(6)"Press SPACEBA
R for next byte"
120 FOR N%=0 TO 511:K%=PEEK(B%+N%)
125 PRINT#0,TAB(7);N%;TAB(16);HEX$(K%,2)
;
126 IF K%<32 THEN K%=127
130 PRINT#0,TAB(24);CHR$(K%)
140 WHILE INKEY(47)=-1:WEND
150 NEXT
160 PRINT#0:PRINT#0,"Another one- Y or N
? "
170 INPUT A$:IF A$="Y" OR A$="y" THEN 20
180 END
500 MEMORY &9FFF:B%=&A000
510 INK 0,0:INK 2,26: INK 3,1
520 CLS:WINDOW#1,1,40,1,3
530 WINDOW#2,1,40,23,25
540 WINDOW#0,5,35,4,22
550 BORDER 4
560 PAPER#1,3:PAPER#2,3
565 CLS#1:CLS#2
570 PEN#0,1:PEN#1,2:PEN#2,2
590 RETURN
600 FOR N%=0 TO 27:READ D$
610 POKE B%+N%,VAL("&"+D$):NEXT
620 B%=&A01C:RETURN
800 PRINT#0:PRINT#0,"Range 0 to";K%;" on
```

```
ly, try again":RETURN
1000 DATA DD,7E,00,DD,56,01,1E
1010 DATA 00,21,1C,A0,F5,0E,07
1020 DATA CD,0F,B9,F1,C5,4F,CD
1030 DATA 66,C6,C1,CD,18,B9,C9
```

Figure 8.1. The track & sector program in BASIC.

the listing will look on the screen as it does here. Be very careful about the DATA lines, because these contain the machine code. An error in any one of these items will cause certain doom, so save the whole program before you attempt to run it. When the program runs, the screen divides into three windows, and you are asked for a track number. The track numbers range from 0 to 39 and on CP/M discs the first two tracks are reserved for CP/M use, with programs. Track 2 is used for directory entries, using 32 bytes for each entry. When you have entered an acceptable track number, you are then asked for a sector number. The DDI-1 Manual shows the usual range of sector numbers as hex #41 to #49, but in this program the sectors are numbered from 0 to 8 only, so as to avoid complications. When you enter a valid sector number you will hear the disc spin, and the display changes to show the byte number, its value in hexadecimal, and the character which corresponds to the byte. Showing the character is very useful when you are looking at text files or directory entries, because it allows you to read the text, even though it is in the form of a vertical column. The display shows one byte, and waits for you to press the spacebar so that another byte can be displayed. You can hold the spacebar down if you want to see the bytes scrolling up the screen – useful if you are looking for something specific. If you don't want to see all of the bytes in a sector, you can use ESC ESC to leave the program in the usual way.

How it works

The BASIC part of the program is relatively simple. After clearing the screen, the subroutine at line 500 is called. This sets up the memory size, the address for the machine code, and the windows. The paper, border and pen colours are also selected. The next subroutine at line 600 then pokes in twenty-eight bytes of machine code which perform the disc access. The bytes are stored in hex codes, because these are easier to enter and check than ordinary (denary) numbers. With this done, the program is ready to start, and the title is printed. Lines 30 and 50 request the track and sector numbers respectively. If an incorrect number is entered, the error is trapped, and a subroutine at line 800 prints a message, so that you can re-enter the data.

When the numbers have been entered, line 70 adjusts them. For a CP/M disc, the sector numbers must be in the range of #41 to #49. Line 70 adds 1 and also #40 to accomplish this. The reason for this rather curious looking action is that it is possible to format a 'data disc' which is not of CP/M format. Such a disc uses sector numbers (hex) #C1 to #C9. If you have such discs, then all you have to do is to alter the first part of line 70 to read:

$$S\% = S\% + 1 + \&C0$$

An alternative would be to ask at the start of the program 'Is this a CP/M or data disc', and assign a variable DT% equal to &40 or &C0 depending on the result. The second part of line 70 combines the track and sector numbers into a two-byte number, with the track number as the higher byte. In BASIC, this is done by multiplying the track number by 256 and then adding the sector number. By putting the number into this form, it is easy to pass its value to the machine code section.

The call to the machine code is made in line 80, and the value of track and sector number is passed. The machine code selects the disc operating ROM, reads the track and sector that has been specified, and then restores the BASIC ROM so that the program can resume. Line 90 then clears two of the windows, and line 100 prints the headings on the top window. Line 110 prints the message on the bottom window, then a loop starts in line 120. This will print the byte number (its position in the sector, ranging from 0 to 511), its value in hex, and its character shape. If the byte value is less than ASCII 32 (the space), then a chequer pattern is substituted. This is because printing some characters whose ASCII codes are less than 32 can cause odd effects, like screen clear, cursor movement and so on. Line 140 tests for the spacebar being pressed, and loops continually until it is pressed. At the end of the loop, you are asked if you want another set of track and sector numbers to investigate, and if you answer with Y or y, the program repeats from line 20.

The machine code

This is for machine code programmers only! The assembly listing is shown in Figure 8.2. The listing has been produced by the ZEN assembler which I use, rather than the Amsoft GENA3, but there is no difference as far as the assembly language itself is concerned. If you use the GENA3 assembler, you will need to use ENT $ in place of LOAD $ in the second line. Lines 3 and 4 get the sector number byte into the A register, and the track number into the D register. The E register is loaded with 0, which is the number for drive A. The HL register pair is loaded with the address of a buffer in which 512 bytes can be stored after being read from the disc. The AF registers are then pushed on to the stack so as to store the sector number which was loaded into A. With the number 07 in register C, the call to B90F will select the disc drive ROM, which is coded as number 7. The same call will leave the BC registers loaded with identification numbers for the BASIC ROM which usually occupies the addresses #C000 to #FFFF. When this has been done,

```
 1
 2                         ORG    0A000H
 3  A000  DD7E00           LOAD   $
 4  A003  DD5601           LD     A,(IX+0)
 5  A006  1E00             LD     D,(IX+1)
 6  A008  211CA0           LD     E,00
 7  A00B  F5               LD     HL,BUF
 8  A00C  0E07             PUSH   AF
 9  A00E  CD0FB9           LD     C,07H
10  A011  F1               CALL   0B90FH      ;select ROM
11  A012  C5               POP    AF
12  A013  4F               PUSH   BC
13  A014  CD66C6           LD     C,A
14  A017  C1               CALL   0C666H      ; read sector
15  A018  CD18B9           POP    BC
16  A01B  C9               CALL   0B918H      ;deselect
17                         RET
18             BUF:        DS     512
                           END
```

Figure 8.2. The assembly language for the machine code portion which reads the disc.

the AF pair are popped from the stack, and the BC number is pushed on. The sector number in A is then passed to C so that it can be used by the next routine. This call is to a routine in the disc ROM, and it will read the sector which has been specified by the track and sector numbers that have been passed in registers C and D. The buffer will then be filled by bytes from the selected sector, and the BC number is then popped from the stack. This is then used by the call to #B918 to restore the BASIC ROM so that the program can return to BASIC.

Copying tapes

The practice of issuing 'copy-protected' tapes is one of the most infuriating side effects of software piracy. Tape is not the most reliable of media, and a backup copy of any valuable tape is a must. Protection systems frustrate attempts to make backups, but have little or no effect on the real pirates of the industry, who can always find paths around protection systems. Fortunately, the Amsoft manuals show in sufficient detail for any machine code programmer how backups can be made. In your case, you will want to make copies of your tape programs on to disc. You can, of course, have this done for you, but this means paying twice for the same program, particularly when you realise that all of your programs will probably fit on to one disc! A very few programs cannot be saved on to a disc because of their length. Amsoft suggest that you can still use these from tape by disconnecting the interface (with the computer switched off) then loading and running from tape. This is rather a desperate measure, and I would not like to keep pulling the interface on and off these rather fragile connectors. The solution is probably to rewrite the offending software so that it *does* fit into the slightly more restricted memory of a disc equipped machine. Very often this only means separating instructions from the rest of a program and storing them separately on the disc.

The program which is described here will allow you to make copies of your 'protected' software in BASIC on to disc. This assumes that the protection system is the one that Amsoft use (SAVE"name",P) and which is described in the *Concise Firmware Specification*. There is nothing illegal about transferring a program which you have paid for on to a disc (which you have also paid for!), providing that the copy is for your own purposes. I hope that when the Software Protection Bill (which is at the time of writing going through Parliament) becomes law, this will put an end to tape and disc protection systems. We can then adopt the sensible system of licensing which is used by Digital Research for the CP/M system disc, rather than making it difficult to back up tapes and discs.

Following that sermon, on to the program of Figure 8.3. Once again, this is in BASIC, but it consists almost entirely of pokes of machine code. The machine code is poked to addresses which lie *below* the start of BASIC, so

```
10 CLS::TAPE
20 M%=325
30 FOR N%=0 TO 40:READ D$
40 POKE M%+N%,VAL("&"+D$):NEXT
50 PRINT:PRINT"Now go through this seque
nce-"
60 PRINT"1. Type NEW [ENTER]"
70 PRINT"2. Type CALL 325  [ENTER]"
80 PRINT"3. Type LIST  [ENTER]"
90 PRINT"4. Type :DISC   [ENTER]"
100 PRINT"5. NOW SAVE THE PROGRAM ON DIS
C"
110 PRINT:PRINT"That's it!"
200 DATA 06,00,21,00,00,11,2B,A0,CD,77
210 DATA BC,30,18,C5,21,70,01,CD,83,BC
220 DATA C1,21,70,01,09,EB,21,83,AE,06
230 DATA 04,73,23,72,23,10,FA,CD,7A,BC
240 DATA C9
```

Figure 8.3. The BASIC tape copy program.

it's not necessary to reserve memory for the program. When the machine code bytes are poked in place, you are asked to carry out a five step plan. First, you use NEW to remove the BASIC program from the memory. This does *not*, however, remove the machine code. You should then use CALL 325 to run the machine code. This will give you the usual tape messages about pressing PLAY, then any key. The machine code has been set up to load the first program that it comes to, so you need to have the cassette rewound to the start of the program that you want. When you press PLAY and any key, the tape will start, and loading looks normal. Note that you *do not* use the CTRL-ENTER type of load in this case. When the 'Ready' prompt shows that the tape is loaded, you can use LIST to prove it. Now use |DISC to switch to the disc system, and you can save your program to disc under whatever filename you like to use – not exceeding eight characters.

How it works

The BASIC part of the program simply pokes machine code into the memory starting at address 325 (Hex #145), so there isn't much to say about it, and we'll concentrate on the machine code (Figure 8.4). The protection system, as the manual informs us, works by reading byte 12H in the tape header. This 'header' is the first chunk of data that is read from the tape, and it is not part of the program. If the header is not read in the usual way, the byte can't be detected, and the protection is ineffective. This allows us to use

```
 1                      ORG   325
 2                      LOAD  $
 3           BASC:      EQU   0170H
 4           PNTRS:     EQU   0AE83H
 5  0145 0600           LD    B,0        ;next file
 6  0147 210000         LD    HL,00H     ;not used
 7  014A 116E01         LD    DE,BUFR    ;2K buffer
 8  014D CD77BC         CALL  0BC77H     ;open file
 9  0150 3018           JR    NC,EXIT    ;out if wrong
10  0152 C5             PUSH  BC         ;save length
11  0153 217001         LD    HL,BASC    ;start address
12  0156 CD83BC         CALL  0BC83H     ;read all file
13  0159 C1             POP   BC         ;get length
14  015A 217001         LD    HL,BASC    ; get start
15  015D 09             ADD   HL,BC      ;find end
16  015E EB             EX    DE,HL
17  015F 2183AE         LD    HL,PNTRS   ;put in pointers
18  0162 0604           LD    B,4        ;four of them
19  0164 73    LOOP:    LD    (HL),E
20  0165 23             INC   HL
21  0166 72             LD    (HL),D
22  0167 23             INC   HL
23  0168 10FA           DJNZ  LOOP
24  016A CD7ABC EXIT:   CALL  0BC7AH     ;close file
25  016D C9             RET              ;to BASIC
26           BUFR:      DS    2048
27                      END
```

Figure 8.4. The assembly language which shows how the copy system works.

some of the other reading methods which don't activate the protection. If you load the header, for example, as if it were for a text file, you will print the messages and show the filename, but without the protection. This header read action is performed by the subroutine at #BC77, which is normally used by the data reading routines (OPENIN). This requires some registers to be loaded. Normally, B has to be loaded with the length of the filename, but if B=0, then the first file on the tape will be read. HL has to be loaded with the address of the filename, which is normally in a buffer in high memory. This can be loaded with any dummy value if the B register is loaded with zero. The DE register is the important one. It has to be loaded with the start address of a 2K block of memory which will be used as a buffer. This is the buffer which would be set by an OPENIN command in BASIC. When the routine at #BC77 is run, it will give data back in these registers, but the important one for our purposes is that the length of the file is given in BC. This quantity then has to be pushed on to the stack, because the next routine may corrupt the contents of BC. If anything goes wrong with the process, or if the ESC key is pressed, the carry flag is set, and our routine allows this to make an escape back to BASIC. With the header read, and the number of bytes on the stack, we can now read the rest of the program into the memory. Since BASIC programs start at #0170, this address is put into HL, where the routine requires it. A call to #BC83 now loads in the rest of the file, starting at the address in HL. Unlike a BASIC program being entered from the keyboard, however, this does *not* alter the program pointer addresses in #AE83 onwards. This, in fact, is another part of the normal protection system. To make the program copyable, we must set these pointers to one byte following the end of the BASIC program. This is done by adding the start address in HL to the length bytes in BC, and poking the result into the pointer addresses. This can be done in a loop, in lines 19 to 23. When you return to BASIC, you will find your program can be listed, and, better still, saved on to disc. It's a remarkably simple solution, in contrast to some of the elaborate tape copying programs that are commercially available for about the same price as this whole book!

Screen recording

It is very often useful to be able to make a recording of text which appears on the screen, particularly items like disc directories, or the printed output of some programs which you might need to recall. For example, it is very useful to be able to record the instructions for a program on disc, so that valuable memory space does not have to be used. A recording of text on a disc which has been made by the program here can be 'replayed' by using the TYPE command from CP/M. This program is specifically for text; it will not record screen graphics which have been made on the high-resolution screen. Because only text is recorded, there is much less memory involved than when a complete high-resoluton screen is recorded or replayed.

```
10 CLS:M%=&A000:MEMORY M%-1:CS%=0
20 FOR N%=0 TO 81:READ D$
30 D%=VAL("&"+D$):CS%=CS%+D%
40 POKE M%+N%,D%:NEXT
50 IF CS%<>9937 THEN 1000
60 CALL M%
70 PRINT"Press TAB to record screen, rea
d with ":PRINT"CP/M TYPE command. You wi
ll have"
80 PRINT"to reload if the machine has be
en reset."
90 NEW
100 DATA F3,21,09,A0,22,D4,BD,FB,C9
110 DATA FE,09,20,3A,F5,E5,21,4A,A0
120 DATA 06,08,11,52,A0,CD,8C,BC,21
130 DATA 01,01,E5,CD,75,BB,CD,60,BB
140 DATA CD,95,BC,30,19,E1,24,7C,FE
150 DATA 29,20,ED,3E,0A,CD,95,BC,3E
160 DATA 0D,CD,95,BC,26,01,2C,7D,FE
170 DATA 1A,20,DB,CD,8F,BC,E1,F1,C3
180 DATA 4A,13,53,43,52,4E,44,55,4D,50
1000 PRINT"Mistake in data- please check
your":PRINT"listing again.":END
```

Figure 8.5. The screen to disc program in BASIC.

The program, Figure 8.5, consists of a short BASIC routine which pokes machine code into memory. There is rather more machine code than in the previous examples, and so a check has been included. This takes the form of the variable CS%, which is the total of all the bytes of machine code. If this total is incorrect, the cause is usually a faulty DATA entry, and you should check your own listing if this error occurs. The listings in this book have been taken directly from the computer printouts, and if you type them exactly as you find them here, you will have exactly the same program as I have. In other words, don't ask if there are any misprints that stop the program from working – there aren't!

When the machine code has been poked into memory, part of it is run to establish connections. This part of the machine code will ensure that when you press the TAB key, whatever is on the screen will be recorded on disc. You have to be careful about accidental pressing of the TAB key, particularly when you have no disc in the drive. You should also remember that this program will be wiped out if you reset (using CTRL, SHIFT, ESC), or if you change the memory allocation to a higher number. When the program is in memory and linked in, a short reminder is printed on the screen. By this time, however, the program has vanished because of the NEW in line 90, leaving behind the machine code, and the message on the screen. When you have a screen full of text that you want to record, make sure that there is a disc in the drive, and press the TAB key. You will hear the disc start and stop, but you will have to wait until the disc has started and stopped *for a second time* before you have a recording. Don't, whatever happens, take the disc out until this second recording is finished. The screen is recorded under the file name of SCRNDUMP, and you should find this name in the disc catalogue. You can replay this file by using the built-in CP/M utility TYPE. You can also change the name of the file if you want to save another screen.

How it works

The program is entirely in machine code, and you should skip this section if you don't understand machine code programming. The listing in assembly language is shown in Figure 8.6. Lines 3 to 7 poke the address of the start of the main routine into a CPC464 jumpblock address at #BDD4. This address is used when a character is placed on the screen, and it is a convenient point to intercept the TAB character. In the main routine, which starts at line 8, the character code number is checked. If the character is not the TAB, then the jump in line 10 causes the normal jumpblock routine to be used at once. When the TAB character is recognised, however, the AF and HL register pairs are saved on the stack, because they will be needed by the ROM screen routine, and our routine starts in line 12. This loads the HL pair with the address of a filename, SCRNDUMP, loads B with the number of letters in this name, and loads DE with a buffer address. The call to #BC8C then opens a file to the disc drive, causing the first piece of disc activity. The HL register pair is then loaded so that the CALL to #BB75 can place the cursor at the top left-hand corner of the screen. The CALL to #BB60 then reads the character under the cursor, and the CALL to #BC95 records the character in the file. This is repeated for 40 characters, following which a line feed and carriage return are recorded. This ensures that the file will be read correctly by TYPE when needed. It also makes for a very simple reading routine, if you design a machine code reading system for use with AMSDOS. The next row is then selected and tested, and the action proceeds until all of the screen rows have been recorded. The file is then closed by the CALL to #BC8F, and this is also the next line that will be used if there is an error condition, including a break. The registers are then restored from the stack, and the program ends with a jump to the correct jumpblock destination of #134A. The bytes of the filename are held at the end of the program, and also the buffer which is used to store bytes until they can be recorded on to the disc.

```
 1 ;
 2
 3  A000  F3              ORG   0A000H
                         LOAD  $
                         DI                    ;no interrupts
 4  A001  2109A0         LD    HL,START        ;of routine
 5  A004  22D4BD         LD    (0BDD4H),HL      ;to jumpblock
 6  A007  FB             EI                    ; restore
 7  A008  C9             RET                   ;back to BASIC
 8  A009  FE09    START: CP    9               ;is it TAB key?
 9  A00B  203A           JR    NZ, EXIT        ;out if not
10  A00D  F5             PUSH  AF              ;preserve
11  A00E  E5             PUSH  HL              ;registers
12  A00F  214AA0         LD    HL,TITLE
13  A012  0608           LD    B,8
14  A014  1152A0         LD    DE,BUFR
15  A017  CDBCBC         CALL  0BCBCH
16  A01A  210101         LD    HL,0101H        ;row, column
17  A01D  E5             PUSH  HL              ; save on stack
18  A01E  CD75BB   LOOP: CALL  0BB75H          ;place cursor
19  A021  CD60BB         CALL  0BB60H          ;get char.
20  A024  CD95BC         CALL  0BC95H          ;record
21  A027  3019           JR    NC,ERROR
22  A029  E1             POP   HL              ;row, col
23  A02A  24             INC   H               ;next column
24  A02B  7C             LD    A,H             ;test it
25  A02C  FE29           CP    41              ;too much?
26  A02E  20ED           JR    NZ,LOOP         ;back if not
27  A030  3E0A           LD    A,0AH           ;line feed
28  A032  CD95BC         CALL  0BC95H
```

```
29 A035 3E0D             LD    A, 0DH      ;C/R
30 A037 CD95BC           CALL  0BC95H      ;RELOAD
31 A03A 2601             LD    H,01
32 A03C 2C               INC   L           ;next row
33 A03D 7D               LD    A,L         ;test it
34 A03E FE1A             CP    26          ;toomuch?
35 A040 20DB             JR    NZ,LOOP     ;back if not
36 A042 CD8FBC   ERROR:  CALL  0BC8FH
37 A045 E1               POP   HL          ;restore
38 A046 F1               POP   AF          ;registers
39 A047 C34A13   EXIT:   JP    134AH       ;rejoin routine
40 A04A 5343524E TITLE:  DB    'SCRNDUMP'
40 A04E 44554D50
41               BUFR:   DS    2048
42                       END
```

Figure 8.6. The assembly language for the screen to disc action.

Note that the program cannot be relocated simply by poking it to different memory addresses. This is because of the use of the filename and buffer addresses. If you want to use different addresses, you will have to make sure that these address bytes are changed. The address of &A000 has proved convenient, however, and it will be only if you are using a very long BASIC program to produce screen text that you will be unable to fit this program in.

Memory display

The CP/M utilities allow you to display memory, but the display is in hex only, and there is no facility for displaying the ROM of the CPC464. This program allows you to see what is stored in either ROM or RAM, and displays the bytes in hex and in character form. The character form display makes it a lot easier to see titles and other text displays. As usual, the program uses a mixture of BASIC and machine code, with the machine code poked into place by the BASIC program. Since the machine code is fairly short, there is no check sum used, and you should look at your own listing carefully to ensure that the DATA lines are correct. It should go without saying that you should always record any program before you attempt to run it.

The program, in Figure 8.7, follows the lines of the track and sector reader. If you have already recorded the listing of Figure 8.1, you can load it

```
10 CLS:GOSUB 500:GOSUB 600
20 PRINT#1,TAB(13)"Memory Display.":PRIN
T#1,TAB(13);STRING$(14,"_")
30 PRINT#0:PRINT#0,"Starting address ":G
OSUB 2000
40 IF ST%<-32768 OR ST%>32767 THEN PRINT
"Mistake in address- please try again":G
OTO 30
50 IF ST%>=0 AND ST%<=&3FFF THEN GOSUB 1
000
60 IF ST%<=-1 AND ST%>=-16384 THEN GOSUB
 1000
90 CLS#0:CLS#1
100 PRINT#1,"Addr.";TAB(15)"Hex bytes";T
AB(25)"Characters."
110 PRINT#2:PRINT#2,TAB(6)"Press SPACEBA
R for next set, ESC to stop"
115 PRINT#0,HEX$(ST%,4);
120 FOR N%=0 TO 7:AD%=ST%+N%
```

```
130 IF CH$="RAM"THEN K%(N%)=PEEK(AD%)
140 IF CH$="ROM"THEN K%=AD%:CALL &A000,@
K%:K%(N%)=K%
160 PRINT#0,TAB(6+3*N%);HEX$(K%(N%),2);:
NEXT
165 FOR N%=0 TO 7:IF K%(N%)<32 THEN K%(N
%)=127
170 PRINT#0,TAB(30+N%);CHR$(K%(N%));:NEX
T
180 WHILE INKEY(47)=-1:WEND
190 ST%=ST%+N%:GOTO 115
200 PRINT#0:PRINT#0,"Another one- Y or N
?"
210 INPUT A$:IF A$="Y" OR A$="y"THEN 20
220 END
500 MEMORY &9FFF:B%=&A000
510 INK 0,0:INK 2,26: INK 3,1
520 CLS:WINDOW#1,1,40,1,3
530 WINDOW#2,1,40,23,25
540 WINDOW#0,1,40,4,22
550 BORDER 4
560 PAPER#1,3:PAPER#2,3
565 CLS#1:CLS#2
570 PEN#0,1:PEN#1,2:PEN#2,2
590 RETURN
600 FOR N%=0 TO 26:READ D$
610 POKE B%+N%,VAL("&"+D$):NEXT
620 RETURN
700 DATA DD,6E,00,DD,66,01,5E,23,56
710 DATA 36,00,2B,CD,06,B9,CD,00,B9
720 DATA 1A,77,CD,03,B9,CD,09,B9,C9
1000 PRINT#0,"ROM or RAM?. Please type a
nd":PRINT"press ENTER key."
1010 INPUT CH$:IF CH$<>"ROM"AND CH$<>"RA
M" THEN PRINT"Error- please try again":G
OTO 1000
`1020 RETURN
2000 INPUT ST$:IF LEFT$(ST$,1)="&" THEN
ST%=VAL(ST$):GOTO 2030
2010 V=VAL(ST$):IF V>32676 THEN V=V-6553
6
2020 ST%=INT(V)
2030 RETURN
```

Figure 8.7. The memory reading program in BASIC.

in and use it as the basis for this listing by editing some of its lines. The subroutine which sets the windows is identical, and only the number in line 600, and the DATA need to be changed for the machine code poke lines. In line 30, you are asked for an address, which you can provide in hex (using '&') or in denary. The subroutine in line 2000 tests to find which has been used, and allocates the correct number to variable ST%. This is not completely straightforward, because the range of an integer number is -32768 to $+32767$, compared with the usual address range of 0 to 65535. Lines 50 and 60 then test the address to find if it could be in the ROM range. If the address is in the range that can only be RAM, between 16384 and 49151, then nothing more is needed. If the address is one that is shared by ROM and RAM, however, you will be asked by the subroutine at line 1000 which you want. You should type ROM or RAM, and then press ENTER. The reason is that the bytes stored in RAM can be looked at by using PEEK, but the bytes in ROM can be found only by using a machine code subroutine stored at address &A000.

The display can then start. The display consists of an address number in hex at the left-hand side of the screen. This is the first address in a set of eight, and the bytes which are stored at this and the next seven addresses are then displayed. On the same line, you will see the character shapes which correspond to these bytes. Another loop is used for this, storing the codes in an array. There is a difference, however, because all bytes of less than 32 denary have been changed to the checker pattern, ASCII 127. This avoids trying to print codes that will shift the cursor or clear the screen. You can obtain another set of eight characters by pressing the spacebar. If you keep the spacebar pressed, the display will scroll steadily, which can sometimes be convenient for looking at text stored in the memory.

The assembly language

Once again, unless you are a Z80 machine code programmer, look away. The assembly language is shown in Figure 8.8, and is very simple. The address of a byte has been passed from BASIC by the command CALL| &A000,@K%. This results in the bytes of K% being stored at an address which is found at IX $+0$ and IX $+1$, and this address is gathered into HL. By using LD E,(HL), the low-byte of the value of K% is put into E, and by using INC HL and LD D,(HL), the high-byte is placed in DE, so that the whole of the address that we want to PEEK is in DE. The high address byte in HL is then zeroed, and the HL number decremented to point to the low-byte. This is done so that we can return a value of K% to the BASIC program as one byte only. Two calls are then used to switch on both lower and upper ROMs, and the load in line 12 will put a byte in the accumulator. This byte will come from the ROM address that has been specified, and by using LD (HL),A this byte is put back into the address which BASIC uses

```
 1                   ORG   0A000H
 2             LOAD  $
 3  A000 DD6E00 LD    L,(IX+0)    ;get
 4  A003 DD6601 LD    H,(IX+1)    ;VLT address
 5  A006 5E     LD    E,(HL)      ;low byte
 6  A007 23     INC   HL
 7  A008 56     LD    D,(HL)      ;high byte
 8  A009 3600   LD    (HL),0      ;zero upper
 9  A00B 2B     DEC   HL          ;restore address
10  A00C CD06B9 CALL  0B906H      ;switch rom
11  A00F CD00B9 CALL  0B900H      ;on
12  A012 1A     LD    A,(DE)      ; get byte
13  A013 77     LD    (HL),A      ;put in VLT
14  A014 CD03B9 CALL  0B903H      ;disable
15  A017 CD09B9 CALL  0B909H      ;ROMs
16  A01A C9     RET
17             END
```

Figure 8.8. The assembly language which switches on ROMs and reads their contents.

for K%. The ROMs are then switched off again by two calls, and the program returns. Because of the use of (HL), the single byte which was read will now exist in the BASIC program as variable K%, and it can then be transferred to an array, like its PEEK equivalent.

Disc editor

This is a program which allows you to *change what is stored on a disc*. Because of that, it has to be used with very great care. You must never alter a disc unless you have a backup copy. The only exception to this is if you are in the desperate state of having a valuable disc which has been magnetically damaged and cannot be loaded or copied. Do not attempt to use this program unless you know what you are doing. Neither I nor the publishers can be responsible for any loss of data due to the use of this program, because what you do with it is entirely up to you. If you know what you are doing, it can sometimes be a way of rescuing a valuable disc from a fate worse than reformatting. If you don't know what you are doing, experiment with a backup disc that you don't care too much about until you *do* know what you are doing.

With that very necessary warning over, let's see what the program of Figure 8.9 does. It is very similar in style to the track & sector reader and once again, you can create one from the other by renumbering and editing. There is much more machine code data, however, so in this case a checksum has been used to ensure that you can call the machine code only when the data is correct. If you get an error message about this, check your data lines carefully. Look in particular for a B used in place of 8, or the other way round, since this is the most common source of trouble. If the DATA lines are correct, the program will display its track & sector title, and you will be asked as before to supply track and sector numbers. If you are trying out the program on a spare disc which has some files recorded, use track 2, sector 0. This will produce the directory entries.

You will now see the same display as for the track & sector program. This time, however, you need to use the ENTER key if you want to proceed from one byte to the next. If you want to change the byte at an address, you type the new byte, *in hex code*, and then press ENTER. This will repeat the line on the screen, to ensure that you see the change, and you will need to press ENTER to get the next line. When you have made alterations, pressing CTRL \ will enter a 'face' shape in the entry strip at the bottom of the screen, and when you press ENTER on this, the sector will be rerecorded on the disc. The whole procedure has been made *deliberately* clumsy, so that you don't find it too easy to zap valuable bytes off a disc! If you want to test it, look through the directory sector until you find a filename. If necessary, press ESC twice and rerun the program when you have noted the start of a filename. When you know the byte number at which the filename starts, you

```
10 CLS:GOSUB 280:GOSUB 390
20 PRINT#1,TAB(13)"Track & Sector.":PRIN
T#1,TAB(13);STRING$(14,"_")
30 PRINT#0:PRINT#0,"TRACK No.- (0 to 39)
 ":INPUT T%
40 IF T%<0 OR T%>39 THEN K%=39:GOSUB 430
:GOTO 30
50 PRINT#0:PRINT#0,"SECTOR No. (0 to 8)
":INPUT S%
60 IF S%<0 OR S%>8 THEN K%=8:GOSUB 430:G
OTO 50
70 S%=S%+1+&40:D%=T%*256+S%
80 CALL &A000,D%
90 CLS#0:CLS#1
100 PRINT#1:PRINT#1,TAB(8)"Byte No.";TAB
(20)"Hex";TAB(27)"Char"
110 PRINT#2,"Type hex. number to change,
 ENTER to":PRINT#2,"ignore, CTRL \ to pu
t back to disc."
120 FOR N%=0 TO 511:K%=PEEK(B%+N%)
130 PRINT#0,TAB(7);N%;TAB(16);HEX$(K%,2)
;
140 IF K%<32 THEN K%=127
150 PRINT#0,TAB(24);CHR$(K%)
160 INPUT#3, K$:IF K$=""THEN 220
170 IF K$=CHR$(28) THEN 260
180 IF LEN(K$)>2 THEN PRINT"Faulty numbe
r":GOTO 160
190 K%=VAL("&"+K$)
200 POKE B%+N%,K%
210 GOTO 130
220 NEXT
230 PRINT#0:PRINT#0,"Another one- Y or N
? "
240 INPUT A$:IF A$="Y" OR A$="y" THEN 20
250 END
260 CALL &A023:REM RECORD
270 END
280 MEMORY &9FFF:B%=&A000
290 INK 0,0:INK 2,26: INK 3,1
300 CLS:WINDOW#1,1,40,1,3
```

Figure 8.9. The disc editing program in BASIC – experiment with backup copies only!

```
310 WINDOW#2,1,40,22,24
320 WINDOW#3,10,30,25,25
330 WINDOW#0,5,35,4,21
340 BORDER 4
350 PAPER#1,3:PAPER#2,3
360 CLS#1:CLS#2:CLS#3
370 PEN#0,1:PEN#1,2:PEN#2,2
380 RETURN
390 CS%=0:FOR N%=0 TO 61:READ D$:D%=VAL(
"&"+D$)
400 POKE B%+N%,D%:CS%=CS%+D%:NEXT
410 IF C$<>7825 THEN PRINT"FAULTY DATA,
PLEASE RE-TYPE":END
420 RETURN
430 PRINT#0:PRINT#0,"Range 0 to";K%;" on
ly, try again":RETURN
440 DATA DD,7E,00,DD,56,01,32,3E,A0
450 DATA 1E,00,ED,53,3F,A0,21,41,A0
460 DATA F5,0E,07,CD,0F,B9,F1,C5,4F
470 DATA CD,66,C6,C1,CD,18,B9,C9,3A
480 DATA 3E,A0,ED,5B,3F,A0,21,41,A0
490 DATA F5,0E,07,CD,0F,B9,F1,C5,4F
500 DATA CD,4E,C6,C1,CD,18,B9,C9
```

Figure 8.9. contd.

can edit this name into something different, like ALTERIT – but not more than eight characters. You have to enter the characters as hex codes, so you will need a hex-ASCII table. A suitable table is included in Appendix A.

How it works

The BASIC program follows the lines of the track & sector reader closely, and the main changes are in the entry of replies. A new window, #3, has been defined for this purpose, so that the prompt for the INPUT step in line 160 does not disturb the data display. Lines 160 to 180 test the entry. It is not easy to make a complete set of tests for a valid hex number, and no attempt has been made to trap anything other than the length of the number and the value. Line 190 obtains the value of the hex entry, and line 200 pokes this in place in the buffer memory. The GOTO 130 in line 210 then repeats the display step so that you can check that the change has been made. If you come to the end of the stored bytes without pressing the CTRL keys, then you will be asked for another T & S, and this will allow you to look at more data without altering the disc. You can also use ESC at any point to get out of any disc alteration. If, on the other hand, you have altered bytes and you are determined to see the disc altered, then press CTRL. The disc will spin briefly, and the deed is done. Use CAT now to see if your disc still works! If you have only altered a filename, then you will see the new filename on the disc. If, however, you have altered the numbers that lie between the filenames, then you can expect anything to happen!

The machine code

The assembly language for the machine code is illustrated in Figure 8.10. It is a straightforward development of the track & sector machine code, and it starts by passing values from BASIC into the Z80 registers. In this case, however, the values are also stored at addresses in the program, labelled as STOR. This allows the program to pick up these values easily when the sector is rewritten to disc. The rest of the read section to line #A022 then follows familiar paths. The new part starts in line #A023. This loads the accumulator from memory, and the next line loads the DE register pair. This puts the correct track and sector numbers back into the registers for the write routine, and the disc ROM is then selected by loading the select number 7 into register C and calling #B90F. The sector number is then transferred to the C register, and the sector write routine at #C64E is called. This writes bytes from the buffer to the disc, and then the ROM select bytes are popped into BC so that the ROM deselect call to #B918 can be made. Once this has been done, the program returns to BASIC.

Last word

These utilities should be of considerable use to you if you plan to be more than a passive user of the CPC464 dics system. Similar utilities will probably be available on disc (at a price!) if you want to avoid the keyboard exercise, but if you are interested in the way that your disc system works, then the description of these utilities should be of interest. We have come to the end of this road now, and the end of this book. The aim throughout has been to introduce you gently to the CPC464 disc system, and to take you through to a stage where you can make very effective use of it. You should by now have reached that stage, and be reaping some return from your investment in the disc system. Most important of all, you have another powerful component of a computer system working for you, and you now know how to get the best from it. If this book has tempted you to learn more about machine code, then you will quite certainly find my book *Introducing Amstrad CPC464 Machine Code* a useful introduction.

```
 1              ORG   0A000H
 2              LOAD  $
 3  A000 DD7E00 LD    A,(IX+0)
 4  A003 DD5601 LD    D,(IX+1)
 5  A006 323EA0 LD    (STOR),A
 6  A009 1E00   LD    E,0
 7  A00B ED533FA0 LD  (STOR+1),DE
 8  A00F 2141A0 LD    HL,BUF
 9  A012 F5     PUSH  AF
10  A013 0E07   LD    C,07H
11  A015 CD0FB9 CALL  0B90FH   ;select ROM
12  A018 F1     POP   AF
13  A019 C5     PUSH  BC
14  A01A 4F     LD    C,A
15  A01B CD66C6 CALL  0C666H   ; read sector
16  A01E C1     POP   BC
17  A01F CD18B9 CALL  0B918H   ;deselect
18  A022 C9     RET
19  A023 3A3EA0 LD    A,(STOR)
20  A026 ED5B3FA0 LD  DE,(STOR+1)
21  A02A 2141A0 LD    HL,BUF
22  A02D F5     PUSH  AF
23  A02E 0E07   LD    C,07H
24  A030 CD0FB9 CALL  0B90FH
25  A033 F1     POP   AF
26  A034 C5     PUSH  BC
27  A035 4F     LD    C,A
28  A036 CD4EC6 CALL  0C64EH   ;write sector
29  A039 C1     POP   BC
30  A03A CD18B9 CALL  0B918H   ;deselect
31  A03D C9     RET
32        STOR: DS    3
33        BUF:  DS    512
34              END
```

Figure 8.10. The assembly language for the disc editing machine code sections.

Appendix A
The ASCII Codes in Hex

No.	Hex.	Char.	No.	Hex.	Char.
32	20		80	50	P
33	21	!	81	51	Q
34	22	"	82	52	R
35	23	#	83	53	S
36	24	$	84	54	T
37	25	%	85	55	U
38	26	&	86	56	V
39	27	'	87	57	W
40	28	(	88	58	X
41	29	)	89	59	Y
42	2A	*	90	5A	Z
43	2B	+	91	5B	[
44	2C	,	92	5C	\
45	2D	–	93	5D	]
46	2E	.	94	5E	^
47	2F	/	95	5F	_
48	30	0	96	60	`
49	31	1	97	61	a
50	32	2	98	62	b
51	33	3	99	63	c
52	34	4	100	64	d
53	35	5	101	65	e
54	36	6	102	66	f
55	37	7	103	67	g
56	38	8	104	68	h
57	39	9	105	69	i
58	3A	:	106	6A	j
59	3B	;	107	6B	k
60	3C	<	108	6C	l
61	3D	=	109	6D	m
62	3E	>	110	6E	n

63	3F	?		111	6F	o
64	40	@		112	70	p
65	41	A		113	71	q
66	42	B		114	72	r
67	43	C		115	73	s
68	44	D		116	74	t
69	45	E		117	75	u
70	46	F		118	76	v
71	47	G		119	77	w
72	48	H		120	78	x
73	49	I		121	79	y
74	4A	J		122	7A	z
75	4B	K		123	7B	{
76	4C	L		124	7C	¦
77	4D	M		125	7D	}
78	4E	N		126	7E	~
79	4F	O		127	7F	

Appendix B
Use of the CTRL Key in CP/M

The CTRL key is used in CP/M along with letter keys to allow a number of useful commands to be entered from the keyboard while a program is running. The actions are listed here. To avoid having to repeat the CTRL key symbol, only the letters are shown, so that **C** means CTRL C. Since the CTRL key prints an up-arrow on the screen, this symbol is sometimes shown in place of CTRL. Another CTRL symbol is the circumflex (^) which many printers use in place of the up-arrow.

C	Stops a program running.
E	Carriage return to screen but not to program.
H	Delete character and backspace.
I	Tab across eight spaces.
J	Generate line feed, end input.
M	Generate carriage return, end input.
P	Switch printer on or off.
R	Erase and retype command.
S	Screen display on or off.
U	Ignore command, move cursor down.
X	Erase command, home cursor.
Z	End input.

Note: The **P** and **S** commands are 'toggles'. This means that you use the command once to switch on the effect, and again to switch it off. You cannot normally tell, except by trying it, what state the command is in, but when you enter CP/M, the toggle commands are set to printer off, screen on.

Index